The Awakening of Dee

The Signs, The Red Flags, and The Escape

Author DeVondia Roseborough

DEVONDIA R. ROSEBOROUGH

PUBLISHER'S NOTE:

This book is a work of nonfiction accounts. Names, Characters, places and incidents are products of the imagination. Or used fictitiously any resemblance to actual events or locals or persons living or dead, is entirely coincidental.

ISBN-10:069299453X Library of Congress Catalog Card Number: In publication data.

The Awakening of Dee: The Signs, The Red Flags and The Escape
Written by: DeVondia Roseborough
Edited: Complete Steps Publishing
Text Formation: Rasberrirose Foundation Inc.
Cover Design and Layout: Dynasty's Cover Me
Printed in the United States of America

Intro

The Awakening of Dee is for anyone who's asleep...

The Awakening of Dee is for the woman who no longer wants that invisible clueless sticker engraved on her forehead; suctioning the life out of her because the signs and red flags she took for granted has disengaged her spiritually, emotionally, physically, socially, and financially. She assumes it's okay since she hopes things will change. Recklessly retaining her in bondage, while brutally killing her further into an empty pit of hurt and desperation. The Awakening of Dee gives her life and the motivation she needs to embrace change and to exhale, despite the circumstances that has her insecure of letting go. The Awakening of Dee comes with an escape plan and more importantly, reasons to stay away from toxic people, places, and things. This book will begin with my story and from my experience, the trouble it caused my life and the cons for holding on. This journey will take you on the road of self-destruction for not fleeing the soul tie that intertwined a messy, yet powerful message that you are about to read. The pages you'll turn will grant you access to my decisions in remaining in a muddle. The chapters you'll explore will explain why my choice to break a yoke that was not ordained by GOD was important for not only me but for women that need the same detachment from their relationships.

In confidence, it will inspire more women that feel like they can't let go. This release of pain, purposely driven by sweat, blood, and tears will motivate women that are secretly dying in an unfit situation and how to make the necessary changes in removing obstacles out of their lives. Without hesitation and with determination, in knowing the difference between intuition and the power of discernment. The Awakening of Dee is an eye opener, releasing those things that have more control over her than GOD. When this happens, nothing in life will be in control without HIM. This is the second release under The Baptized N' Warm Milk Collection based on Temptations of the Flesh. It is necessary for us to go through things I'm sure. But we as women must stop allowing the presence of a man and how he makes us feel top priority over our self-worth, belief system, and self-respect. The time is now and I welcome you to The Awakening of Dee.

Author DeVondia Roseborough

Chapter One

The most amazing day of my life was December 2013. I was sitting at my computer and I noticed a message from someone who looked very familiar to me. The man who used to maintain my yard alerted his presence with a simple greeting of hello. I hadn't seen him since he cut his feet on the blade of his lawnmower in 2009. He sent me messages that sparked my interest and I was intrigued in knowing how life has been treating him. He didn't look the same as the days before. He was a lot heavier, a strong bone structure with three moles strategically, placed on the left side of his face. However, his features had changed. It bears so much pain to write about my happiness that was swiftly taken away from me. I must admit my standards did not allow me to come close to him as soon as he would have liked me too because what he presented to me wasn't the man I once knew. The first thing I asked him after his many advances were, "Are you still married?" Of course, he said no and had gotten a divorce and was no longer with the woman that I knew he was married to during my lawn cutting season. I pondered many days and nights if I should give him the opportunity to take me out. I had no idea what I was setting myself up for. His messages began to get intense and as I scaled back more, I would find myself on his Facebook page checking him out and sizing him up.

He did not have the perfect set of teeth in his mouth, he had lost a lot of weight, compared to the man I remembered pushing the lawn mower and cutting down trees. The only reason why I accepted the opportunity was that I felt like GOD had presented an opportunity for me to love and be loved. Or was it GOD? Since the 2003 HIV diagnosis, I felt for many years' no one would want me. I mastered several dates and even relationships that failed of course. Hey, everything is not meant to work out. This guy was the epitome of a man. Let me slow down, I'm getting ahead of myself. I felt like a burst of zeal had begun to connect with my writing. A boost of energy replenished my deserted being; as my mind pondered the beginning of it all.

I cried with hard thick tears of, 'How could I have allowed this to happen to me?'

He pursued me and I responded with many, "I'm busy", "I'm talking to my kids", or "I'm in a relationship", indirectly suggesting the timing was not good. The only reason it had the truth; I wasn't sure. I did not want to fall into what I had just got out of, with a man with many lady friends and conversations filled with lies that I could discern right through. I swiftly began to annul that situation before it started. Now here comes Mr. Fantastic with everything I had dreamed of right before me but not in the physical. I was not attracted to him physically at all. I prayed to GOD to relax my desires and humble my acceptance as I'm forced into a mandatory praise and worship down

I-85. One fine morning as GOD began to speak to me; I was sure it was not the voice of a stranger, HE told me, "How dare you place stipulations on people knowing how you felt when people rejected you because of the diagnosis". You will see as I speak on HIV I do not claim it. I call it the diagnosis and possess no ownership of the disease. After turning him down numerous times, I decided to give him a call and asked him out. The first thing he said to me was he did not have a car. I've dated men before who did not have a car but he was quick to say he had a job. That was a plus. I didn't have any plans on taking care of a man but I remember the days when I was that type of girl. I'm a woman now. I invited him out to lunch the first Saturday in January 2014 and it was the most amazing lunch I ever had with the opposite sex in years. I looked across the table at him as he ordered his meal sizing him up some more. We sat in a nice booth at Red Robins at Northlake Mall. I could see the potential in his eyes and as I searched a little deeper and without a word spoken, I could see the hurt this man was carrying. But I could not determine where he was in his life with this hurt. As the conversation began, I saw beauty in his eyes. After I complimented him, I was suddenly attracted to his boyish-like shyness that made him blush from my immediate affirmations I supported

him with. He loved being affirmed. He asked me the sweetest question I had ever heard. You know that one-liner that woo you but you still hold your guards up so high you attempt to lower the playing field so you can enjoy the moment. He asked me in gentle yet baritone sound, "How long do I have you for?"

"How long do you need me for?" I politely responded. His candid response, "Forever".

As my heart melted my intimate body parts began to feel a vibrating sensation that I squeezed my legs and giggled with excitement.

The night was still young and the rain decided to continue as he picked up where we left off, he said, "Since we can't decide on forever, let me have you for the rest of the day". He was a complete gentleman. He paid for the meal, waited until I was seated before he sat, opened doors and put his coat on my shoulders as we made our way to see Anchorman 2 at a nearby theater. Yes, I remember everything. I remember the good stuff. We always do. But we fail to recognize the signs until it's too late and then we must go through the process of eliminating and weighing options that don't want to cooperate with our feelings. The movie was a choice I would not have selected but it ended up being a great film; to say the least. We went back to my house for a drink and one thing led to another and boom he was so energized he walked home while I rested my pretty little head. Yes, I will be candid but will leave more to the imagination. He became my sun up and my sundown. The doors continued to open for me, the chairs were always pulled out, and we dated like teenagers meeting one another on summer vacation for the very first time while hating when the other went home. Our time together was worth more than being apart. He was married when he was cutting my grass in 2009 and I was not her hangout buddy or this is my girl to his ex-wife. However, she was a Facebook friend. I knew they were divorced because he said so. Our days and nights were spent spoiling one another with kisses, hugs, to slow dances in the middle of the living room. He has a majestic sound that rings from his baritone voice. He loves music like I do and he has a great eye for wording his lyrics to the emotions he sang about. That all by itself gave me life. Sitting back writing on his days off or after work, listening to free beats on the internet and coming up with lyrics to express his passion for me. This kept a smile on my face. I felt secure with him and we talked many times about the diagnosis and his very words were, he never cared about what others thought of him and he was a man, a man that makes his own decisions. My curiosity to why he wanted to be with me was no longer a mystery. He spoke frankly about my chocolate dark skin and how beautiful I was. I knew I was beautiful. I cultivated long ago from the stage of being validated by anyone. It felt so good to hear him tell me I was smart and beautiful. This is what attracted him to me and on top of that, he only had two requests of me. The first request was to show him how it felt to be loved and do everything that GOD has called me to do. He was not concerned about the diagnosis and he told me that many times. After I would inquire about how he felt being with me, he would say that he did not see the diagnosis. He saw a beautiful black woman who he'd fall in love with. Me being who I am, would not allow him to catch the bus to work. Everything around us was convenient. Where he lived and where he worked was minutes away, literally minutes. When he told me he could cook, I knew I had hit the jackpot. We took turns cooking for one another and shared many evenings in the kitchen cooking together. He was not chagrined of me and he was adamant about confessing his love for me on social media. The people were very happy for me as he would say; they didn't give a hoot about him. What I had to explain to him on numerous occasions that I have a story that has impacted my community since the day of the diagnosis. Many follow me because of the inspiration I give despite my circumstances. I told him to not get caught up in likes but be grateful for the salutes from those we discern were genuinely happy for our relationship. , everyone was not happy about our new-found relationship. The days and nights were splendid. The first Valentine's Day I ever had in love, since Jermaine gave me roses in 2002. He was not skimpy on the gifts either. A nice Michael Kors handbag, candy, teddy bear, a card with a bottle of wine in a cute red bag with lots of I love you written on it. He closed the night out with dinner by candlelight in an intimate setting at P. F. Chang's China Bistro. This was the best night ever in the history of Valentine's Day.

Chapter 2

February 2014 the snow was melting and we were snowed in for a couple of days. Him being an outdoorsy person was exciting for me. To walk hand in hand with the white fluffy substance that will soon melt by the rays of the beautiful sun that shined so brightly over my life during this time was everything. It was drawing nearer to his birthday and I wanted to do something very special for him. I dare not share anything he put out about the demise of his marriage because one thing I know is certain; his story, hers and the truth. Plus, it was none of my business, yet he shared his reasons with me. Something began to nudge at me and from the looks of some of her post on Facebook, I had every right to feel the way I was feeling. I asked him so many times was he still married and he continued to say no. He assured me there was nothing I had to worry about. Then one day I received an inbox message from the ex-wife to give her a call because, "As the mother of his children and his wife, I feel we need to have an understanding". The first person I called was my cousin Ebony to ask her how I should handle this. "Yeah, call her and don't come off all wrong. Hear what she has to say and go from there". She said. I marinated for a minute and then I gave her a call. She was not rude nor disrespectful. She even told me she respected my ministry and what I did for women and girls in the community.

She went on to say how she did not understand how he did not tell her about he and I being in a relationship. She had to find out about it on Facebook.

"He could have told me it was you the lady that had the dog name Butta", she said.

She asked me if he told me that they were trying to get back together prior to me. The only thing he told me was there was a trip to where she was and it was not a good visit and she confirmed that. The next piece of information she delivered was one of the records.

Because of the caddy subliminal post, I felt she was in her feeling because of the goodies he spoiled me with and the good times we were sharing on Facebook was not sitting well with her and her self-confessed.

"Here he is up there taking care of you and my boys are feeling a certain type of way because he is not doing for them". You know I pumped the brakes and said, "He sends money when he gets paid and it's been times when I have given him money back he has given me to send to the boys". She went on to say, "I knew you were not that kind of woman to be with someone who would not take care of his kids". She expressed her delicate self even more by telling me she had a man on hold because she and him, the man I had fallen in love with would reconcile. Her boyfriend told her clearly, he has moved on and so should she. And I interjected that he was right. If a man wanted to be with you he would be where you are and if he really wanted to be with you, you will be where he is. She let me know they were still married and that she had asked him why he had me

thinking they were divorced when they're not. He had
told her that I had looked the divorce up online and
could not find a record of it. Which was true, I couldn't.
She wanted to make sure it was okay for the boys to
communicate with their father since we were now a
couple and she said these very words, "As long as he's
happy I'm happy. He has a good heart but he's a big
liar. I will give him the divorce with no problem".
He denied all of what she had said. But I kept it in the
back of my mind and told him I needed to see the proof
and I needed to know when and where they were
married. From the East Coast to prison, from West
Virginia to somewhere else. I can't remember all the
places the nuptials supposedly took place. All I knew
was he had the justice of the peace on the East Coast
very busy. Still, I could not find any record of the
marriage. We had a heated altercation and I even put
my paws on him because I knew he was not being
honest with me. Nevertheless, he knew how to assure
me, that I had nothing to worry about. It stayed in the
back of my mind.

Chapter 3

Meeting family members, going on super romantic dates, making love like we were newlyweds who dared to be unattached from one another; except for work and school. I was a full-time student at a local university and I promised myself when I made the decision to go back to college that I was going to finish what I started. I couldn't remember the last time I felt so complete. He wanted so bad to be in a relationship and he made it clear that he did not want to be alone. He talked so much about what he wanted our future to consist of and when he gets his license back, all the traveling we were going to do. I anticipated the moment because the dreams he shared were the visions I longed to engage in with the one I loved and who loved me. His desires were to have special individuals in his life together for his birthday and I made it happen. I tell you he smiled so hard all I could do was smile back at what he never had before in his life. He was finally happy. Multiple individuals were in my ear on how happy he looked and how his past was dark and they were happy he had finally found the joy he was missing. It did not last long. The last female that had her heart wrapped up in him found it her business to make it known she was a woman scorned. I did not have to do anything or say anything because he had people and I had people that believed in us and went for her as she came for us. I remember being awakened out of my sleep about 3:00 A. M.

A dear sweet Facebook friend saw a post the woman scorned left on a picture he and I were tagged in. She informed me that she had insomnia and could not sleep and she felt it was her right to make me aware of the foolishness taking place while we slept. She went on to say how messy women are when a man no longer wants them. To be honest I had no clue of who she was and why she had it out for me was obvious. But why? This was crazy. I let him know and he said he would take care of it. The problem was, he was dealing with a woman with no home training and I did not take well to the random outburst she displayed on social media. Especially, when it came to her posting on my business page. The attacks became toxic to my relationship. I was sitting in class one day and my phone kept pinging. My cousin was calling me to let me know what was going on. I checked the Facebook page and it was a hot thread of "He has a woman now"

"DeVondia is a real woman"
"…No bruh did not get her a promise ring. LOL". I chuckled and continued to allow them to handle my light work. I had no time in wasting my words on someone who was clearly in distress for him and I being a couple. I kept myself far away from the nonsense until she posted obscenity and vulgarity on my business coaching page. My trusted executive assistant LaFewanda caught it, called me and it was deleted. Again, I let him know and he said he would handle it. I was down to my final straw.

I rarely checked my messenger's spam, other, and archived messages. On one day, I sat in my living quarters cleaning out my spam and unwanted inbox messages. This was the first time I had noticed messages from one of her (The woman that was leaving messages on my page.) friends, letting me know that she was not trying to come between our relationship but he has a baby on the way but she was not having it. I knew then that it was a trick. I also knew I was too old for this imprudence. Challenged in my flesh and ready for war, I responded. Yes, I did. I let her know don't come for me and my man anymore. Do what she wanted to do, we good. I was every fat bitch she could think of. Of course, I let him know what went down, just in case he decided to handle it. My words will end up being invitations to an opportunity that cause for immediate hands-on of a good old-fashioned butt whooping. I continued to keep in a close part of my mind that I have more to lose. He in turns gets upset with me for retaliating. His solution to everything is nothing. Just allow it to die down and leave it alone. No! He was running from everybody and everything that was a problem in his life. This is what he had become accustomed to. Not confronting what was not working in his life. Soon enough, the blocking was in effect and peace was reestablished. Temporarily that is.

Chapter 4

I was, giving more of myself to a man that was not honest with me. I knew he was not straightforward, but I loved him. As time progressed, the combination of good food, sex, and hot dates continued to keep me in a place of ooh, ah, and yes, while distracted from the big picture. The fact here is, don't be fooled by what a man can do. A man is supposed to take care of his woman but baby not when he's married. It was nothing for him to peel off $100 bills, followed by the words, "Do what you want with it". And on top of that, he paid bills, kept my car cleaner than any Pacifica on a dealerships' showroom floor; cooked dinner, cleaned up and fixed what was broken around the house. But inside I was committing an assault on my mind, body, and soul; broken into a million pieces, with no architect in sight to repair the remnants of my disaster. Timeless efforts were made for me to demonstrate to him what it felt like to be loved. By this time, we were an item. The Facebook couple who gave hope to many that desired the relationship we exhibited. We had the smiles, the right outfits; my hair defined the upkeep of our love because a kept woman is a woman worth keeping. Marching around in my symphonic rhythm in love. No, let me rephrase that too drunk in love. Cooking up a mess not realizing the recipe was spoiled from the start with lies and deceit. One thing for sure I ate well. I became annoyed by things and even people in his life.

I never wanted anything more for him and me but love and happiness. I know that my power of discernment is real. I had an unction that things were not right. Even though the truth had presented itself, I needed more and I wanted more of him. I craved the way he treated me. Queen is the highest esteem of royalty; I'm living in falsehood and against the royal priesthood I'm entitled to.

"Will I ever seek the truth" is what I asked myself? I was going to church faithfully every Sunday. Well, I tried. When he and I got together that was an important part of keeping our relationship on the right track. He spoke frankly about his reasons for not wanting to attend church and I respected the church hurt story. Then he decided why not. That Sunday he decided to go to church with me was the weirdest feeling in the world. I felt hot as if hell was a part of the service. I told him lets go around to Pastor's office so I can introduce you. Even though they knew one another I wanted him to meet who I had fallen in love with. When my Pastor opened the door to his office I could see the displeasure on his face. He said these very words to him.

"You went from driving a Pinto and now you are driving a Cadillac. This is a good woman right here. Take good care of her". I did not understand but they shook hands and Pastor said, "Do not worry about what others are going to say or think". I understood that part very well. I went out the office somewhat relieved. As service began to start and it was time for the word. I noticed a change in the atmosphere. I felt the need to be vigilant and began seeking immediately what was wounding me. I had a feeling that the word Pastor was going to preach was about me. I cannot tell you the chapter he came from or the subject of the sermon. I do remember these words coming from the pulpit, "Why is she..." and he spins around with tears in his eyes. "...with someone else's husband". The sermon was on point I'm sure. But the words that he said associated with his message had my toes crushed so bad, toe cast was needed to repair my bones broken.

"How you over there mowing someone else's grass and your grass needs to be cut".

I dropped the microphone for him. A big flag on the play and I stayed in the game. The ride home was a quiet one. The pit of my stomach was increasing the invisible embarrassment that secretly molested my insides from the church parking lot, down Beatties Road and into my driveway. I sat in the driveway with a solemn look on my face with no response to his statement, "Church was good". He walked around to open the door for me and asked me, "What's wrong baby?" I was convicted by the message. He had no idea, or did he? I went in and came right back out. I had to say something.

It would not be right if I didn't. I wanted to know if he felt convicted. Of course, he said no. I didn't feel right. I explained to him the importance of living accordingly. I asked him one more time before I went in to change out of my church clothes, "Are you still married?"

"No, DeVondia.

Chapter 5

It was getting close to Mother's Day 2014 and the tension was so thick around the house that it was ridiculous. I was trying to figure out why he's so distant and why I'm acting so sensitive. I have never had an overly sensitive man in my life. After hearing his childhood issues; I decided to be more understanding. I dare not share his stuff. That's his story to write. I was tired of the off balance of the relationship. The hours on his job were cut and he was spending more time away from me than trying to mend what was already a diabolical mess. I remember going to get him from his aunt's house and he had an attitude with me because I felt like I needed to know his whereabouts.

"As your so-called woman and the dangers in the streets, you should want me to know", was always my response. See, he had this thing about not being able to do life like everyone else. Going to prison does not stop anyone from living life after they return home. He could not channel the anger and pain he experienced and had to blame the closest thing on him to bear the hurt of his past, me. The Friday before Mother's Day became a shouting match and the day I officially slapped the black off his face. He was tired of me questioning him about being married and I was tired of his mendacious rebuttal. I was ready for the truth, at any cost.

All I remember is clothes were thrown across the room into suitcases and liquor bottles were thrown at him. As he walked out the door, I threw a basketball and hit him square in the back of his head. He was angry and his friend picked him and his pieces up from my driveway and whisked him away. A night of crying, screaming and trying to make sense of why I was so upset with a man that was not honest with me. I was in love with another woman's husband and like the meme says, "God is not going to send you someone else's husband". I'm crying like crazy, about to lose my everlasting mind over another woman's husband. I pacified the situation with the fact that they had been separated since 2009. Many of my choices led me back to where I escaped from, full circle. I was back in the saddle again. I called my daughter. Let me tell you about my daughter Makeeba Jackson. She is my oldest daughter but she is older than me. We lean on one another for advice. We tend to get through our storms by having one another lifted in prayer and answering the phone when no one else wants to hear what we must say. I let her know what was going on with her pops and she immediately let me know, "I can look the divorce up for you. It's public records ma". I knew this, but how, was the magic question for me. I sent her their names and she hit me back within seconds to let me know everything but the time of the wedding. My heart sunk and I was finally faced with the reality of my discernment. I hope you're paying attention to the signs.

Yes, you. Oh yes, I cried some more and was distraught from the information she not only found for me, but I shed more tears after I received the screenshot she sent me via text. I fell into a mild depression. Feeling hopeless, pondering repeatedly the question, who is going to love me now? If GOD did it before there's no question that he will do it again. A couple of days went by and I was watching the 5 o'clock evening news and I received a call from him. He wanted to talk face to face and I agreed. I went to pick him up. Again, a man that did not have keys to anything was getting ready to get in on the passenger side of my car and have something to say that would turn me back from whence I came.

His words were, "DeVondia I love you and I have not been honest with you, I'm still married. I lied to you because I knew you would not have given me a chance if I told you the truth".

I looked at him and told him, "I already knew". He went on to say, "I talked to her". Now whether these are true words or not.
I am telling you what he told me.

"I talked to her and I told her I was in love with you and she said as long as I'm happy she was happy". He asked for forgiveness and we kissed and made up. Here we were having our first makeup after a breakup.

Chapter 6

The summer of 2014 had hit and it was time for my infamous fish fry and cookouts; entertaining my soul with the music blaring from the speakers, as life continued to exist at 3615, we made the most of what we both felt was promising. Things appeared to be on track but it was hard for me to forget being lied to. In my younger age, I was the president of taking care of a man. I was raised by a loving father who deposited the importance of how a woman should be treated and how one is taken care of. He exemplified the essence of a man that does right by his woman. But I didn't pay any attention to it until I saw that in whom I fell in love with. I never had a man to take out the trash without having to be told. Not ever did I have a man to pay my bills and lace me with designer things and made sure my wallet kept something green in it. I did that on my own. But it felt good. He always tucked a nice one hundred bills in his wallet for a just in case moment. He taught me not to worry about today and let tomorrow take care of itself. He wasn't afraid to get his hands dirty. When the oil needed changing in my daughter's cars. He was a well-skilled laborer with many attributes that made me feel as if I had finally hit the jackpot. When I began to see a difference in the relationship was when he was asked to go on the road long distance with his job.

I had to ask my mother how she did it. Being that my father was a retired truck driver. I needed to incite on how to be patient and wait on my man. The farthest thing in my mind was what anyone thought. I did not tell too many what I was dealing with. But the select few that did know could either relate or supported me in whatever decision I made. I can't begin to count how many times I pondered leaving this man and starting my life over without him. The devastation was not so much with him, but me doing me the way I did me. I deserved better. I settled for less. Trust was an issue because I knew if he lied before that he would continue to do so. Plus, she told me, "He has a good heart but he's a big liar". She knew him better than I did. The signs were there from the beginning. Nevertheless, I neglected the opportunity to flee. I wanted so badly to be loved; I corrupted the life within me set aside just for this divine purpose. Not realizing, I was killing my ministry. I felt disconnected in giving him what he asked for in the beginning. I was all about doing my thing. My education was not up for discussion with no one. My honor roll status was smarter than the decisions I made. I guess it was because he gave me something no one else was bold enough to do. I emptied my heart, secrets, and even tears on the effects the diagnosis took on my life. Again, he saw a beautiful woman. He said he knew what he was getting himself into when he came for me. He was not afraid and did not care what anyone else thought.

He needed me to stop thinking so hard and enjoy the relationship, wholeheartedly It was kind of hard to do. So, after being lied to, why couldn't I have that boldness in this situation? I lacked the control of my appreciation of being single again. It felt good being in love. Even if it meant being in a relationship with a man that was still married. I even tried to justify the reason for their long separation. Never compromise with wrong. You will never win.

Chapter 7

Washing, ironing, cooking, and cleaning, it had to be too good to be true. Now I'm seeing a difference in the things that need taken care of in the home. The trash was secondary. The yard was not tended to as he frequently did before. The lovemaking had no substance and half the time I was just there. What is really going on? I felt we spent a lot of time together and this was straining our relationship even more. He had moved out numerous times just to move right back in. The simplest thing sparked the most sensitive responses from him till I was getting tired of trying to rationalize with a grown man embarking upon 40-years of age. I needed help. I remember purchasing the book the 5 Love Languages but I couldn't find it. I went to the bookstore and repurchased a copy. I began to sit in silence; reading in the living room, in the back seat of the car, and even during a relaxing bath, I found after reading the book he needed to be affirmed.

"Honey, thank you for taking out the trash".
"Honey, I love the way you cut the grass".
"Babe, you did a wonderful job on that dinner, please, thank you, I love you, you are special…" I wanted to scream. I never had a man that was so needy. Then is when I realized, if he was built for me, I would've been equipped for that. Now shut this book but remember what page you were on.

We know what we have no business doing but we go against what we know we're not supposed to, to have our mind, body, and soul wrapped up in a journey of twist and turns. I was living life, wondering when this paperwork was going to take place and how we were going to get things popping for this wedding. Yes, he asked me to marry him. He told me that he loved me and he wanted to marry me and spend the rest of his life with me. He would ask me to promise him to never get sick on him and die. He said he did not know what he would do if something was to happen to me. "You are my balance", he said. I understood that. I was much smarter than he was and he admitted it many times. That was his major attraction, besides my beauty, he would tell me how smart I was and I began to question what the need was in telling me something I already knew. There was no need in challenging the truth. But I began to grow concern when he would tell me he had never had a woman as beautiful as me. "Women of your caliber do not even look at me", he would say. I tried to give him insight into things. However, I made him feel like I was treating him like one of my coaching clients. It got so deep that I stopped responding. Either way, it was an argument drawing a larger wedge between us. After the first couple of runs on the road, we felt it was something we both needed. With time away from one another it had gotten so bad, I would miss him when he was gone and wanted him gone when he returned. He would say what I was thinking and I knew then we had something more in common than I realized. One run of him on the road I noticed our conversations were shorter and we argued over whatever. I sensed the division and would always question him with, "Who is she?" Of course, he would say, "Nobody, you don't have nothing to worry about". But I knew better. When he was home the trash was not taken out, the grass was neglected and the sex was just a job to do to keep what was left straight with the woman he said he loved. Out of the entire time that we were together, he called after a heated spat to apologize and asked me something he never asked me before. He wanted to know if he had anything to worry about when it came to HIV. I wanted to know where this was coming from. I already knew someone was in his ear. I had assured him he was good with me and on top of that he could either go to the health department or I can have one of my testing and counseling buddies to come to the house and test him in private. He brushed it off, while I continued to feel like something wasn't right. The conversations we used to have while he was on the road no longer had time for me. He knew when to call and he knew when not to answer. To be disconnected from a man I had no connection with left me feeling powerless. However, my power of discernment was warning me of the chaos that was getting ready to take place. I remember reading something that said, "Don't get caught up in a man more than your relationship with GOD". I was trying to build an affair on shaky grounds with a man that was not my equal and neglected praying and asking GOD for guidance. I was too busy praying for the relationship to work out and taming my mind to say the things I needed to say instead of what the Holy Spirit was discerning within. I wanted it to work so bad that I manipulated my own walk with GOD. Remember to never get caught between a man and your purpose. Time progressed and picking him up from work was no longer an option. It was, "I'll let you know". It was always an excuse when he didn't come home.

"I'm with my cousin".

"I'm watching the game".

"Dude you don't even hang with him and you don't even like sports like that". Okay, I settled. Until one day we were about to make what I thought was love and I smelled the scent of rubber on him. Now mind you, we had not had sex in a minute and there was no way a condom scent should be lingering from the man that said it was nobody else. For a minute, I thought it was the wife back in the picture and I even told him to put his family back together and leave me alone. He even called her to verify the situation on several occasions. She even told me, "I want this divorce just as much as him". I needed to know who she was. I felt it in the pit of my stomach and every morning my cousin Ebony and I would try to dissect the situation. Until I received the call I was waiting on.

Chapter 8

As I walked through the kitchen I noticed once again the overflow of trash. I was accustomed to keeping house. However, with a man in the home, it was necessary for him to pull his own weight. I had a lot of discrepancies in this relationship. We cannot pick and choose ones' friends but I did not care too much for the company he kept. The only reason I felt disconnected was that I was on another level of expectancy when it came to my surroundings. If he was happy, it didn't matter until he made comments on how he felt certain ones were not treating him fairly. You know what I mean, reciprocating the same value of friendship he ignited. When he hurt, I did too. , I had no win trying to let him discover what my discernment revealed. When it came time for him to face the reality of it all he was mad at the world and I was right. I'm still not secure with the fact that someone else was now in the picture. I was not convinced of the lies that continued to spew from his mouth. I walked around like I knew and even vocal about my revelations. I was even hopeful in marrying the atmosphere that I would receive a call or come face to face with this unknown distraction. We decided once again to have separate addresses but shared the same zip code. This meant we were not too far away from one another. Nothing kept us apart from one another but work, school and in the cut of my-mind; another woman. We fussed more when we were in one another's company but when we were apart we had the best conversations. Until it was time to discuss how I felt about me knowing he was seeing someone else. I wanted something to eat one day. I had an unction so deep that things were headed in a direction I did not want to face. We can love someone so much and we truly know we need to let them go but continue to force a change in an unvarying situation. He'd begun to have this mystery rides home from work. I was no longer needed. Some of the rides turned into walks home from a homeboy's houses. For someone that did not have a lot of friends, the friend list increased with the lies. Tossing and turning in my stomach; I knew it was time to act fast to save the last little bit of relationship that was inside of me. I knew he loved me but he was disconnected due to me no longer giving him the attention he desired. I made the call stating I wanted to go out to eat.

He said, "Okay".

After surveying the background, I asked, "Where are you?"

With heavy breathing, all he could reply with was, "Going to the store to get some cigarettes for grandma". Now one thing I knew for certain, the grandma I met did not smoke cigarettes. He tried to switch it up and make me think it was his maternal grandmother, whom I had not met. I knew better. I told him I was riding to where she lived but he made it clear that he was not there. I went anyway not concerned about gas. One thing for sure, I did not have to worry about being on empty. I was depleted emotionally and very concerned about the few bucks of emotions I had raging through my body. He said he would call me when he got to his house and I did not believe him. After numerous attempts in trying to connect with him, the phone kept going straight to voicemail. I unblocked him from Facebook. Let me sidebar her… In the beginning, I did not even know that we were friends on the book and then suddenly, we reconnect and in each other's arms confessing love, marriage, and dedication. We had deleted, befriended and blocked one another so much that it was best we were not friends on Facebook. When I unblocked him on this peculiar Monday evening, I was searching for facts that could confirm what I was speculating. I left it unblocked and had further thoughts to go back to it later. I decided to go and talk to someone very close to him. I expressed my feelings on my knowing that it was someone else.

Her response was, "Really?" I looked deeply into the conversation because much was revealed.

She shared this with me. "I had my nephew staying with me and he had other women knowing he was still married. The women would get in their feelings and would be upset about him not being honest. I told him one day, you need not have these women out here like this knowing you are going back to your wife". She very well could have been talking about her nephew but for me, it was confirmation that she knew her son better than me. After I left in tears, I knew that it was time to make a move. I would always call my Ebony for new information. She was my sounding board and gave excellent advice on what to do next. As I'm sitting here typing this I'm simply amazed that my remembrance is so candid and on point. About 15 minutes after I got in the house and off the phone with Ebony, I receive a call from him saying he was ready. I did not hesitate to redress and touch up the MAC, grab my purse and keys and jump in my truck and head in his direction. I recall being on the phone with my friend Toi. As he enters the car I was hanging up.

The first thing that came out my mouth was, "Who is she?"

He let me know, "DeVondia if we are going to talk about this I can go back in the house". I was attentive to this statement. For a man that did not want to be away from me all sudden had someone else to fill a void that I was not fulfilling. All I wanted was honesty. We left for our date at Wild Wings in the Epicenter in Uptown Charlotte. Yes, I continued to express my thoughts and the importance of when this divorce was going to take place. After ordering my glass of Moscato and he a Bud Light; he sat beside me in the booth. I looked out the window onto the deserted 4th Street side of the building, not realizing my attention was not really in the moment. He would tell me to share what was on my mind and to stop thinking so hard. When I finally took control of my mind, I relaxed down and began to have a good time. After leaving we decided to go for a walk. The late-night air was a bit too much so we headed back to the house and him asking me, "Is it okay if I spend the night"

"Of course. Why not", was all I could say. "Under one condition though, I needed a full body massage".

He replied in his deep baritone voice, "Anything for you baby". We get back to my spot undress and had some pillow talk. As soon as he mounts my back for my full body massage, my phone rings. I looked at the clock on the cable box and it said 11:15 P.M. I take crisis calls in the midnight hour so I'm under the assumption that I'm needed. I asked him to get my phone which was turned face down on my DVD shelf beside the bed. He passed the phone to me and I said,

"Hello". The woman on the other end asked for DeVondia. Of course, my name was not pronounced correctly but I corrected the pronunciation and this is what she said.

"You don't know me. I wanted to ask you what you know about him". Now, my marriage to the atmosphere became one and it was now time to go down the yellow brick road and through Alice and Wonderland with the woman that was trying to take my place.

Chapter 9

It was a long time since I had a woman to call me and ask me about a dude I was dealing with. He continued massaging as I asked, "What is it that you want to know?" Her approach was respectful; unknowing to what she had gotten herself into because of the rumors she had encounter and all she wanted was the truth to it all. She too felt he was not being honest. So, instead of going through what she said and how I replied, I will simply list what she said:

- She was told he was engaged to a woman with HIV
- I lived in Rock Hill
- They went and got tested at the health department
- I was beautiful with a short haircut
- She met the boys
- He brought his sword and toothbrush like he was moving in
- He sucked her toes
- She sent him to the store to get some cigarettes
- She knew when I called he jumped
- She didn't have time for foolishness
- He helped her with bills and took her and her kids out to eat at Golden Corral
- She found me on Facebook.

As the exchange of conversation is going, I put the phone on speaker and he slithered off my back onto the bed looking towards the TV. She was introduced by individuals close to him and of course I was the topic of conversation. That's why he came to me about getting tested. It hurt me the most being hugged and kissed on but not respected by the very people that once showed me that they loved me. Now, he lets me know they were talking cold cash junk about me, but hold up. They don't know me, He does. I live 4 minutes away from him. I never lived in South Carolina. I'm a city girl. We have established that I am beautiful and never needed the validation of my beauty or my intellect. Meeting the boys was a shocker to me. This was getting serious knowing he came over to the ex-wife's car to pick up his miscellaneous items he was creeping with. I had no other choice but to let her know he was still married. Coming at me about what a man did to you is a sure way of knowing he sucked my toes too boo, polished them, got them done, all that. He's supposed to. Even men should work what they got to get what they want. Now the pack of cigarettes he was purchasing was for her and him. I heard him asking the clerk for a pack of 100's and a short pack of Newport's. I knew he smoked 100's but the shorts, let's say grandma didn't smoke them and when I asked his mother she confirmed her mother didn't smoke either. When I called he jumped but the majority time he was jumping up in down in her when he was not answering my calls.

I think he's at home or at work. Nah, he on to the next. Neither one of us had time for foolishness. I know you are wondering what he is saying, nothing. I said to him, "Babe you don't have anything to say? Babe, you hear her? She said you sucked her toes. Damn babe, you were over there taking folk to Golden Corral. Chile, he knew better not to take me to Golden Corral".

He took me one time and never again. My questions were simply this:

- Did you two have sex
- How did you get my number? After we got off the phone I told him to get his shit and get the hell out of my house. He told me he was not going anywhere. You're getting up out of here as I slid my pretty sucked feet in my bedrooms' slippers, grabbing my housecoat and asking him, "Did you have sex with her?"

I recall the rubber smell he had on his body during one of our encounters.

"Of course not, she was like one of the guys. We smoked together and chilled on the porch".

"Born at night and my mama said she was watching Flip Wilson while she was in labor with me and I know this was a joke. So, if I was to call her she would say the same?"

"Of course", he said. I called her for the first and last time with those exact questions.

She said, "Yes we had sex but with a condom. I ordinarily wouldn't have called another woman. But because of the known diagnosis, my sister said this was nothing to play around with.

We went together to the health department to get tested and so happen he gets missing today right before we were to go and get the results".

"I wanted to go out to eat so he took me to dinner", was my reply.

"I bought him a pack of cigarettes and he claimed he had no money". She let me know she went on his Facebook because she had just become friends with him. She remembered him saying his ex-wife and I names was similar and she saw a post that we were tagged in. Those that know when you unblock someone everything that was there comes back to life. From relationship status, comments and even pictures tagged. She went through and finally saw my picture and came to my page. I had a video message up on HIV and she watched it, complimented my beauty and said my house was nice. She saw pictures of him and I and confirmed her intuition. My number is on my page of course for crisis calls, book coaching, and business but of course, it was there for a greater reason that night. She was on the speaker again as he and I sat on the porch. She asked where he was. I replied, "He is sitting next to me.

She said, "Looking stupid, right?"

I looked at him laughing, "Yes", singing from my mouth. he ended the conversation about him helping her take care of some bills, giving her his check and that he helped her out during a time of need. I looked at him and said, see what you got yourself into. After I got off the phone he had the nerve to ask me what I was

going to do. There wasn't too much conversation. I
said what I had to say and sent him walking home in
the rain. I called my oldest daughter who is older than
me and let her know what had happened. I cried with
so much pain and anger by the time I spoke to my
cousin Ebony my eyes were swollen and my voice was
hoarse. Luckily, I did not have a class that evening
because I was a complete mess. I screamed, cried, and
I wanted to die. How could the one that loved me hurt
me this way? No, I'm not talking about him. Why did I
not move off the discerning factors that led to the
moment that caused so much emotional distress? I
pulled my closest girls in on it and after many Sundays
of not attending, I even went back to church. I prayed
and went to the altar thinking I left the pain behind.
But it was too much to forget. I still felt the dagger in
my heart. I still felt the anger in my tone. I remember
my Pastor telling me I deserved better and that the
relationship was built on lies and deceit from the start.
He informed me that no one should come between me
and my relationship with God. I was empty inside
worrying about my finances that were all over the place
and I had more bills than money. I was ready to be a
blessing even more to others but it seemed like I was
stuck in a hole. Here I am trying to get back to the
perfect single woman. I have said it before, I have
perfected the single life baby. I know how to do her
well. I didn't want too, but I did. So, I developed a
concept to get single ladies together and have drinks at
least once a month. I pumped it up and I had about six

ladies to come out to one of my favorite spots, TCB 54 Hundred Bar & Grill. I had a ball. On the ride to drop off one the ladies who lived down the street from my ex's best friend; I was blocked coming out of the neighborhood. He had seen me come in to pick her up and was waiting for me to get back. I had a book signing the next day and after we talked and made mad passionate love he accompanied me to my signing. My oldest daughter was mad. She vented about my decision as well as to call her friend and discuss what I felt was my business.

"This is my life and what I choose to do with it, is my business. If you don't like it move out". I meant every word. Live long enough you will see what I'm talking about. Many make choices and decisions that affect those around them and in my feelings, she and no one else mattered. All I knew, it seemed right, knowing it was all wrong. I received calls after I had posted our picture on Facebook from someone who didn't understand my decision. I owed no one an explanation. I knew he loved me and I loved him. No matter how stupid I looked. I was a fool in love. After the signing, we went to eat at his favorite spot and I brought up the divorce issue again. He called her and we talked about 30-minutes about what the next steps were going to be. It went from no one had the money to knowing they could possibly get it done for free. Then came the information about a lawyer and again, she wanted it just as much as he did. We never had bad blood we were cordial and the boys; who I adore started spending the day with us then eventually it was weekends. This was something he truly enjoyed and it made him smile even more. The strength of the relationship began to turn in another direction. He began doing everything he was supposed to do. We were back to fine dining, date nights and enjoying one another without distractions. Until I realized, I was in the wrong place with the wrong person; steady trying to convince myself I was not using him.

Chapter 10

My attitude was on fleek. I did not want to be bothered and I was no longer attracted to any moments of him. The holidays went by and I purchased him something my grandmother said never to buy a man because time will run out. Not knowing, I wanted the time to run out but I was afraid Mr. Sensitivity would cut his wrist if I gave him the boot. It was nearing a year to the day he made me his lady and around the corner was the start of the New Year and I had told him I did not want to go into the New Year with him still being married. I was planning an extravagant wedding on a budget. The red, black and white wedding was going to be after five with seven bridesmaids and groomsmen. I was looking religiously online for venues, participating in bridal showers and entering a contest with notifications on winning prizes for about 8 months straight. One evening, I had a prize that required both the bride and groom to be in attendance. He made some excuse and because he was not cooperative, the 4 day 3-night vacation was forfeited. I had selected my maid of honor and matron of honor. My wedding was going to be elegant and classy. I wanted the church to be filled with those who truly wanted to be in support of the union and the thing I was excited about was being a wife more than the actual wedding. The ceremony was going to be limited to 100 of our close family and friends. After I saw the overflow in the trash can, me wedding binder and ideas went in there as well. I slowly threw away all the items I collected from bridal shows without him knowing. Yet, he would say "You know I'm going to marry you DeVondia?" As if he really could. I must admit I loved the way he said DeVondia. No one has ever said my name so perfect and with compassion as he once did. Here I am sipping on wine and dreaming with my eyes open but in the forefront of my mind I was holding on to empty promises with an ounce of hope of when will this be over, the relationship that is. We rang in the New Year with his friends and saluted the occasion with hugs, kisses and lots of drinks. As smoke filled the air I took notice that I had accomplished another year's journey and only because of the grace of GOD. I called my children and my mother and then we continued to engage with his friends until it was time to go home. I cooked pancakes, Amish-grown turkey bacon, eggs and served my man well. The next day we cleaned up and prepared our day with music, love and us. I should admit we had this social media presence that had many admiring what we had. I know because of the conversations with those that confessed their feelings to me. In the beginning, it was so good. He had no problem with sharing his heart, attaching his words to pictures as he tagged my name inviting affection towards the one he loved, me. He was one that deactivated his page more than anyone I knew because he felt no one showed him any love. One thing you can't be in a relationship is jealous of your mate.

He admitted to me that he was jealous of me and I was in total shock that he admitted it. I refuse to be in competition in my relationship with a male or with my female counterparts. It's enough world out here for us all to make it happen. Being an established woman with my own house, car, bills in my name and not my girls doesn't make me deserve a pat on the back. This is simple responsibility adults should not mind handling. Suddenly, he became accusatory. He would ask me if I had another man and continued to distrust my use of social media. I promise to whoever willing to hold my right hand up I was faithful. I should not have to prove countless times, opening my inbox and showing my post that I'm not out there cheating. I can't help who comes for me but what I do with it aligns my respect for my relationship. I've never cheated on anyone that I was committed to. I had no reason to. Sometimes I've pondered the opportunity with many pursuers but in the end, I respected my relationships. As time drew nearer to Valentine's Day it was time for him to pack his clothes once again and move on. We were arguing more and more about him not trusting me. And here I am wondering why his reply to why he was still friends on social media with the women that were problems in our relationship was a justified confirmation of their request, bull shit. After giving his behind some real talk from the woman that had his back he called me from work and let me know he had deleted them. It made me smile but at the same time, I'm wondering what in the hell is wrong with this dude.

He had a problem with me knowing so many people. He began to hit me with this line, "If we don't make it, it's going to be hard for me to get into another relationship. Everybody knows me as DeVondia's man". I knew what that mess meant. You know I wanted to go there with some choice curse words but I opted to not print them. Of course, I let that slide but I did respond. It will not be the last time. He knew what he was getting himself into, remember. Here we go again the revolving door of, it's over I'm tired. Here I am in respite care in my relationship, pacifying the pain of not knowing which way to go. I knew I loved him but I was extremely tired but not tired enough. I had many conversations with my best friends about what was going on. I connected with warriors and I disconnected from the church. I was tired of playing the two. I have not been to church and when I did go, I attended to not return. All while draining the energy inside; my light dimmed even more. I have a voice that sparks attention, conversation, and hope for not only women but men as well. During this breakup, I looked around the house for all the things he had given me and was indeed thankful. It began to feel like when it was time for us to split, it was right before bills were due. I knew his schedule and the check stubs so it was not a problem. I was going to make a way. However, I had gotten used to him taking care of me. I was strapped for cash and I had to do what I had to do. I had to get a loan at a pawn shop. I even sold my Michael Kors handbags and some other things to make ends meet.

During this time, I connected with my first love. We shared DM on Instagram. I made it my business to solicit his support in co-writing a book about our young and in lust relationship. He went on to voice his agreement on writing the book. He inquired about my relationship. I allowed him in and he expressed how he didn't like it. Anyway, you know how that goes. As I settled being recommitted to the single life, it took me by leaps and bounds. I began being dependent on whichever way the wind blew that day for comfort. I received a call from my first love and we began to talk candidly about what we wanted to write about. We had planned on going to lunch soon to cover this in detail. But the news he told me gave me a blow to my heart. I don't want to get into too much of this but best believe I was hurt bad. I struggled with that thing. Here I was hurting from the last man I fell in love with and the first man that I ever loved has broken my heart once again. When a man has your heart, many things can happen; you can either rekindle the flame, continue to hurt from the pain or allow it to drain you until you're empty and numb. I did it all. I opened myself up to rekindle the conversations that made me feel like I was 17-years old once again. Can I get a break? Better yet I needed to take one. I took a lunch at The Cheesecake Factory one day and the waiter was so fine. I had to get a picture with him. After posting it on Facebook with a sweet message, here he comes ringing my phone. When you love someone love them. Don't wait until you see a stranger with them who means absolutely nothing makes you realize that she loves you but… I had met a couple of guys. One was a trucker and the other a hardworking man. I had more interest in the man who was hardworking than the trucker. My reasons were pure. The trucker really liked me. He was a complete gentleman. The hardworking man was deemed more special. He made me laugh more. The hardworking man invited me more into his world. I decided to go see him after an invitation was presented to go down South and spend the part of spring break with him. When I say I had a ball, please believe me. I was single. I was entitled to have a good time with someone that was digging me and me him. We had the best conversations and we looked forward to seeing one another again. I continued the conversations with the trucker as well. I had a dinner date with him. I asked my friend Toi to accompany me. Never mind why just understand how important it is to not do dates alone with people you meet online. I was getting bored with him because I was more intrigued by the down South hardworking man. But my ex-was not far away plotting when he would make amends. It was always him saying he was leaving. It was always me telling him to get out. It was always me begging him not to go. Then it was him returning to the vomit. It was the end of March and his birthday had just passed. One sweet day I showed my friend a text he had sent me and I accidentally called him. He called back and my friend passed me my phone. I let him know that I called him by mistake. Was it a mistake? He texted back to let me know he loved the sound of my voice. We continued to text back and forth until I got tired and I finally gave in to talk to him over the phone. He wanted to come over and spend time with me. He wanted to confess his love and apologize for hurting me. He wanted me to know that he was willing and ready to work on this relationship. He had paid all the tickets off but one was holding him up from getting his CDL license back. He even went as far to let me know they had filed for divorce and it was a matter of time, that part of his life would be over and we could go ahead and get married and enjoy the love we have for one another. I asked him who he had been with during this break-up and he said he was going, to be honest, and he let me know he had been with the woman he cheated on me with. Apparently, she said something to him that pissed him off and he ended up back home. He said it was over and he was not into her. He just enjoyed smoking reefer with her. He had much to say but that's how they do to make you feel like you matter when you already know you do. My worth in who I was, was on the sales rack. How dare I am a woman of worth with worthless attributes behind closed doors. My demons, my secrets, and my damaged spirit were demolished. I was officially settling. We made the best of the off and on again love affair. He asked me what I wanted to eat. I told him I wanted some pizza. He drove me to Lexington, NC for some Godfather's Pizza. If you have never had Godfather's Pizza, get you some. On the way back, we decided to go to his best friend's house.

It was not that simple. I felt as if they did not want me back at their house because I had called the police on him to get him out of my house on one of our many off and on again, spats. We both were sick and with the flu. He got better but of course, my challenged immune system took some time to get healthy again. My professors understood and allowed me to make up work from my bed. I was so grateful for that and the first time I ever saw a Black man receive a ride in a police car to where he wanted to go, instead of the 4th Street Mansion; the Mecklenburg County jail. The officer lets me know that because he had stayed with me so long he did not have to move out and I would have to file eviction papers. The hell he says. We ended up going to his friend's house anyway. I felt they had no issue with me coming. It was him that didn't want to look bad because he was coming back to what he said repetitively he was through with. He said there's no place you can't go and you already know I don't mind. Everything seemed fine until the thickness of the air became even chunkier, that a chainsaw was needed to cut through it. I paid close attention to the details of everyone's behavior. I noticed his friend asking his wife why she did not handle a call on the phone. She said she did not know anything about it. She was busy preparing what was necessary for her life for her child. The men were in the kitchen hovering in conversation when the doorbell began to ring. No one in the house answered it. I guess the doorbell rang and knocked by itself and answered too. I felt whoever it was really wanted to get in. You know how on every set you find that one who laughs at everything. Yes, there was one. I watched him and the others. His friend goes out the door and a few minutes later my man tells me he will be right back. I asked where he was going and he said across to street to a friend's house. My spirit was already tainted but my discernment was on ten. I picked up my phone and text him, "You think I'm stupid". I knew she was out there. I looked at the table and saw his phone was sitting there still waiting for him to reply. I told the wife I must get something out my car. I grabbed my keys and headed to the door. When I went out the door I saw him walking away from where he said he was going.

I asked him where he was going now and he pointed up the street by the stop sign and said, "To see what she want".

I said, "Who?" And he said her name. The woman he cheated on me with. What in tarnation was she doing up here? Some men mess up by taking anybody and everybody to their hangout spots. If they have no meaning to you then they should not have access to your honeycomb hangouts, period. Especially, where you take your woman.

Chapter 11

I made steps towards him as he made his way to her. Her argument was why she had not heard from him and what was up. He simply stated, "I'm back with my lady and that I understand him, he loved me and we were together again". He was nice enough to introduce us. I simply replied with, "I remember the voice". She was quick to say I had nothing to do with this. She was right. This was his mess he built.

"So, you went back to AIDS?"

"T-cell 700 and viral load undetected", I replied.

Let me set something straight here because I lied to a couple of people stating I cursed that woman out. I only told you what my flesh wanted me to say during this time. However, The LORD told me to stand still. I have more to lose than to be on the street with my name and my character on World Star and any other social media platform acting ignorant. He let her know I did not have AIDS. She went on to let me know that he had been over her house for the past couple of weeks and was talking junk about me.

I told her, "That was to be expected. I did the same thing in his name". She managed to slap him about five to seven times. I admired the fact that he did not hit her back and even told her to do what you got to do. He didn't feel it, so he said. I know the smacks hurt. She asked, "When did this happen?"

We both answered, "Last night".

She came back immediately with, "After I dropped you off?" In between the answers to the questions, her hand so seriously smacks his face repeatedly. A woman scorned. By the last smack, I was 30 feet from them and was tired of the encounter. I hollered his name out and told him to come on. She went her way and he came in my direction. His pride was sick. I told him these exact words after asking him if he was alright.

"Listen, babe, I know you probably are embarrassed right now. People are outside and much more may be watching out of their windows, yet you showed those that raise their hand to a woman that you have self-control. We can do one or the other. We can go downtown to the magistrate office and take a warrant out on her or you can let it go". Of course, he declined going downtown. I told him don't allow your pride to make you feel a certain type of way. I felt like I was winning. I never been in this type of situation before. I have been crossed up though but not like this. I wanted him to know that this isn't the life. It could have gone another direction. I have more to lose and I truly don't have time for it. For the record, I repeated this to him.

"You are never to allow a person that don't mean nothing to you full access to you and your whereabouts. Every woman has no business knowing where to find you. Especially, when you know you love me and I know every spot. I don't claim to hold the keys to the city but I guarantee they know my name". He was uneasy about the situation for the reason being, his pride was crushed. That's what you get when you want to get the life back you lost. He always said he came home from prison went straight to church and got married. He did not get to do the things those he connected with experience in their past. I always said he was lucky. What matters is you have another chance to continue to live the right way and not try to go back to what is now played out. We went back inside and everything was alright. I tried my best to keep his mind off it, just like I did, knowing he went back to the same chick. I had many questions I wanted answers to. I wanted to know if he cooked for her. I needed to know how he had sex with her. I told him, that he better answers every question I had to satisfy my inquisitive nature. He did not want to answer anything but he did. I complicated things even more by asking him to do me like he did her. He didn't want to but I made him with the lights on. I wanted to see his face. I wanted him to see mine. I made all types of demands and dared him to not do so. The trash was taken out before it was needed. My car went back to being showroom ready and when I come home from class I had dinner ready. I reciprocated my duties as well. I admit I got very lazy. What got crazy was I felt like this relationship was super over when he cheated. I became complacent. I stopped cooking, tending to his affirming needs of love language and I even went as far as to change the hardworking man's number in my phone to Minerva. We occasionally had conversations but that was about it. I was tired of feeling lonely in my relationship. He felt the same way. I was not tending to him. However, when I smelled something that was not right I would straighten up. All jokes aside, he was a great provider and I've never had a man to take care of me the way he did. In the back of my mind what I didn't want to do is use this man for my benefit. The things he said were becoming hurtful. I was numerous bitches, but I came back with my favorites. Yes, I can be Samuel L. Jackson's daughter and Bernie Mac's niece in 2.2 seconds flat. The moving in and moving out, the name calling and disrespect we imposed on one another was a clear sign, things were done. Yet, we could say in a few minutes I love you, kiss and make up. He had complaints about not doing anything for himself because he had to pay bills. Well, that's what responsible adults do when they live together. They take care of the necessary so when the time comes for more we can be ready. We made plans to go on a cruise and sail the waters, to move into a condo uptown and live according to our love. I was looking forward to the day our talks became reality. He even knew I loved him when he was away but did not want him here when he arrived. He was adamant about not going anywhere and continued to think he was gassing my head upon marriage. I had thrown everything away. By this time, I had forgotten who I selected as my bridesmaids. I had a friend sending me stuff to look at and she had no idea she was happier than I was. He was tired of my sad face and wanted to know how he could make me joyful in this relationship. I always responded with I was okay. I had become dependent on him, I needed him around, and I felt safe with him; even though I had fallen in love with who he was, not the man that was now before me. The disconnection was piercing to my soul. I no longer desired sex from him. I had an excuse. I even lied and told him I was assaulted while he was away on the last break up. I told him which was true that I had Cancerous cells in my pap smear and I no longer desired it. My mood began to swing from the East to the West and I knew from the partial hysterectomy that the onset of menopause was invading my private parts. The enemy had a problem with that. Chaos stayed relevant between him and me. It was never-ending. At times, I felt depleted and became more emotional. I would cry because my soul was breaking down and I had no fight.

How dare I allow a man treat me this way?

How dare I treat him the way I treated him?

GOD is my source of power and I was losing every watt allotted. I couldn't withstand the force that was keeping me from breaking free. I began to pray. I lost my desire to communicate with GOD. The Spirit and the flesh were at war and I was the one losing the battle. I could not mix the two. I could not hear HIS voice. I felt I was too far away.

I began to pray at night and even when he mouthed off and thought I wasn't listening, my clear reaction was, "I'm praying". This is the man that told me I did not have to work. He had complaints about how unfair it was not to be able to take care of me the way I deserved to be. He wished he had it like he used to. I had no speaking engagements on my schedule and the ones I did have I had to take them because I needed the money. I was tired of negotiating my worth and then hearing sidebars from individuals that couldn't afford to pay me and having something to say about me charging. We all are trying to eat and I refused to starve. If I went to school he was fine with helping me out. He wanted me to stay in school. Then he started complaining in a subtle way. My book sales were down, my coaching clients that came through had already paid for their services. I was undercutting myself, doing business all wrong. I partnered with UBER, a rideshare program. I love it. Not him. He wanted to know who I was seeing and asked me am I cheating, every time I came back from driving. I was applying my make up one morning and he was agitated. I asked him what was wrong and he wanted to know why I was getting so clean. I chuckled of course. I remember him putting a Facebook status up about it. I told him, I never know when I am going to be asked for an interview. My mama raised me to step out the door as if I was expecting something. I will look presentable because I like looking how I'm looking.

He came up and grabbed me and said he loved me. I told him I loved him too and to stop worrying. I saw the tables turn. In the beginning, he was encouraging me to stop worrying about being loved and accept the fact that he is doing just that. Now, I'm telling him the same in a shade tree version. I was a force of patience behind the man I fell in and out of love with. Note, there's a difference between being in love and loving someone. I loved him but was out of love. Sometimes, I didn't even know he was even here. I was in my room or home office while he was outside on the front porch. I knew the life of the relationship was draining him because he had no desire to sing and write music. I would empower him in that way and answer any questions until he said I made him feel as if I was one of his clients. I could tell him something and he would not take it from me. But let someone else say the exact same thing and he would agree. He told me one day I don't have to be right all the time. If I am, I am. We as women should not dumb ourselves down to appease one who is not as knowledgeable as we are. Instead of taking whatever I said as a teachable moment it was another argument. I would have to remind him of one of the major attributes that attracted him to me. "I am smart boo".

Chapter 12

You may wonder what type of relationship the wife and I had. She and I were very respectful to one another. On one occasion, I was having my second fish fry of the year and he had called about his back hurting. I was making money, so I could not excuse myself from my fundraiser. Plus, we had a split and it was a need in me feeding into what I knew what was going to take place. Later a car pulls up with him in it. She was dropping off her husband, the sick man. Like I said, we spoke, laughed and had no hard feelings. At least I didn't until one day I was calling him and he did not answer. Me being who I am. will do a pull-up. When I pulled up she was dropping him off. To no avail, he was honest about the reason but my response warranted why he couldn't have let me know ahead of time, he made it seem like he had something to hide. I even had a conversation with her and like she said, "I do not have any interest in going back. However, if I did, that's still my husband". I never had any more issues with how I felt about them being together after that. The love I have for his children will always be in my heart. I enjoyed spending time with them. They even told their dad I reminded them of their mother. As you can see there is nothing much more to tell.

Chapter 13

I would go to church every now and then. Even went as far to go back to my first love, singing in the choir. I tried my best to go to church on Sundays but it was hard, knowing I had a man at home laying in my bed on a day he didn't have to work. That was one of the reasons he could not go. But his main reason was church hurt. I was tired of looking in my Pastor and First Lady's face letting them down. So, I felt God knows everything anyway so I will just talk to HIM and read my word after my home-based praise and worship. I became better at praying more. He even joined in at times. He was confused and didn't want to mix the two either. He is well-versed when it came to the Bible, being an ex-deacon and armor-bearer and all. We were sinners living an immoral life and I had begun to realize the ways of my wickedness. I still was not ready to go back to church. I needed time to be officially free from this mess before I headed back to the house of GOD. I know that HE will accept me just the way I am. I feared being turned over to a reprobate mind. I would go out UBER driving and would have the best prayer and praise, then come home filled with joy to a house full of wickedness. How can you go out and have peace on the road and be one with GOD and then come to your own house and the enemy sits impatiently on the porch waiting on you so they can have something to fuss about? Our luck was getting even worst. He lost his job.

I supported him and encouraged him as much as I could. Until the innermost parts of my being would scream at me so loud that only I could hear it. Telling me not to do this, don't work yourself to death and have this man sitting around on you. The only thing I could say was, "He was there for me". He held me down and I would not dare turn my back on him. I was running my car in the ground as my $150 apiece 20' rim tires needed to be replaced. My oil needed changing more frequently, the cost of gas was killing me and on top of that I was paying all my bills. You should pay attention to get an understanding to all of this. GOD made away every month and there was no need for doubting him now. I had to call my best friend Tipp for some money and I felt a certain type of way, is that we both felt like there is no need in him being around if he can't help you. Then there are the ones saying this is a test. You two are about to get married and you must look at it in that way. I thought about that but GOD did not send me someone else's husband to marry me, wife me, call me boo and babe and live romantically in my house while we struggled. We were all out of order and GOD was not pleased. Here I was robbing Peter to pay Paul with Moses' gun. When he wasn't looking for jobs on Craigslist, he gave plasma and even had a gig with a temp service that ended up being a waste of gas. I respected his hustle for trying. I just felt he was not trying hard enough. When am I going to get a break from it all? We were not doing anything fun and fun for him was sitting in folks' house chilling. Nah boo, I needed stimulation. I never thought that I was better than anyone else but I desired more when it came to entertainment. I even threw out free opportunities we could engage in. The park and the lake became a pleasant past time until an argument erupted. The simplest thing would set him off and I was quick to head back to my vehicle ready to go. Sometimes we could resolve the issue and sometimes it was a silent ride back home. I know I deserved more. If it wasn't him having something to say about what I'm doing on campus, it was bound to be something else. He complained about me tending to his needs. What it boiled down to was, he did not have keys in his name he and felt I had the upper hand. I told him plenty of times to handle his business.

"Don't talk about the car and apartment you want. Go get it". I put up with a lot but I bought a lot to the table. I was needy. I desired extra attention. I needed to be held and caressed. I wanted my feet massaged. I wanted my nails and my feet did. I no longer got the wants because we could not afford to keep my extra stuff up. One thing my mama taught me if you can't go and get it done, do it yourself. I took the nails off and headed to the beauty supply store for my weave and glue and made things happen; all while I was grabbing his clippers from under the sink and cutting his hair and sending him to the barbershop when it was feasible. He even had something to say when I used the money he gave me back to him.

"Does it matter?" I would let him know.

"One thing you don't have to worry about me doing is messing up money buying clothes, shoes, and hairdos when we have bills to pay".

"These are your bills. I don't have anything in my name at 3615". I was tired of hearing that. It seemed as if he wanted me to feel sorry for him or something. I wanted to get out of this pitiful sinking sand that had no means of letting up no time soon. It was time for my 2015 annual fish fry and I was amped. He handled some things for the fish fry and agreed he would do the frying. The Friday the fish fry started his period came on. Dude had packed his clothes and put them in the middle of the front yard. Luckily, I had no customers at the time and my best friend had pulled up and helps bring things in because he had decided to come off his cycle and agreed to help me out. I sent him out on a delivery and from the moment on the weekend was good. Things went down even more after that.

"Where is my money going?"

"Why am I finding it hard to stay afloat?" As soon as I get things caught up the next billing cycle is back in my mailbox. I started writing another book that will drop after this one titled, Passion in the Pews. This book is based on affairs women have in the church with men of the cloth or with men that sit in the pews who are in relationships. I began getting my me back and was diligently writing. I was still doing what I loved, helping my book coaching clients and not allowing what I was going through to affect that. Still trying to

pretend like I was in love and even invaded my
Facebook and Twitter with my king and my pictures. I
was responding politely and positively to our dead
relationship. Still hoping it was going to change. The
pieces of me were scattered like ashes. I was breaking
down and my pride would not allow me to confess my
innermost commotion. Now, I am dealing with
Keratoconus in my left eye and double astigmatism and
mild cataracts in both my eyes. I was back and forth to
an eye specialist trying to figure out what was going on
with my vision and here I am forced to wear a pair of
glasses with a very old prescription until I could raise
the funds to get the special made Scleral lenses required
for my condition. Another hit in my already drained
pocketbook. At this point, it was not about another
woman. It was the finances that were killing us. I had
thoughts on pawning things again and even had to
resort to doing so. I felt like a man I should not have to
struggle because one thing I didn't do was struggle
alone. I began to explain to myself that this is how it's
going to be until I break free from what's constantly
showing me, that this is not meant to be. I knew his
secrets, I knew his hurts and the pains of his past. I
couldn't begin to explain how much my heart would
not allow me to break free. I needed him and he needed
me. On a bright and sunny day, I was uptight about not
having gas and he would tell me not to worry about
today and let tomorrow take care of itself. I began to
allow this statement to be a part of my daily thought
process. He told me that I had more friends than he did

and I could ask my peoples for money with no problem. What made him think that I wanted my family and friends to knows that my man was not working and I was doing it all? I was selfish with my pride and I did not want to exchange my warfare with anyone; not even my friends and family members. I did not want them to be disappointed in me. I was praying more and more for a breakthrough. I knew this was not going to take place until I escaped from what had me hostage. He even had the nerve to tell me he had me where he wanted me and that I wasn't going anywhere.

Chapter 14

Well to no avail my prayers were answered. He got a job. This job was going to take him out of town. I was okay with that and I felt if there was going to be a revival in this relationship, the away time would give us time to miss one another. The week prior to him starting the job he made me feel like he needed to rest. "Dude bills are still rolling in, we need you on a set making some moves". I was not used to this. I decided why not. I had already degraded myself enough in this relationship. I was watching hardcore porn to pretend to be excited about the sexual encounters that were boring. It was no longer meant for me to be in this travesty but I held on for the rest of the rope that was slowly wrapping around my neck. I knew I had an older sister, Edwina and I had met her one time a long time ago. She found me on Facebook and has loved me ever since. Between her and my niece CiEra, I was smothered in new love from women that were needed in my circle during this time. I and my man, and my sister and her husband went out to breakfast one morning and she was telling me that her husband; my brother-n-law cousin had passed away and they were going to Wilmington NC for the memorial service. I expressed how that would be a nice getaway, but we were financially strapped. She said Y'all should come and asked how we felt about driving my car. Again, we don't have it like that to go out of town.

She let me know we did not have to worry about anything. I mean nothing; hotel, food, snacks, gas and anything I opened my mouth for. They were a complete blessing to us. My only request was, I had to go to the beach and they agreed. We drove down the weekend of the 4th of July 2015. In my mind, this will be a great opportunity to get this relationship in order. Initially, he did not want to go. He felt some kind of way having someone else showing love to us and not being able to do anything for me if I saw something I wanted. I told him don't worry about that. We need to go and have a good time. He finally decided at the last minute he was going, which I knew anyway. The first day was cool. The next day is when the planet tilted. We got into a heated argument so bad that he packed his clothes and left the hotel. I rode around looking for him but he was nowhere to be found. He finally came back. We made love but it was not the same. I went out one good morning to UBER and I let him know that I'd gone by to see our daughter, that is older than us in the hospital. He had a flat-out attitude, making a disclaimer that he knew it was my car but I had something to say when he wanted to go out. I did have a problem with him using my car and then sometimes I didn't care at all. But when you are not meeting me halfway you do not get those privileges. I was the Queen of the snatch back. We went to the movies and he was pissed at me spending too much on popcorn and a shared soda. I was so frustrated I threw the popcorn and screamed, "I'm sick of this!"

He told me, "You can get your money back and we can leave". He did not really want to do this. He became affectionate and wanted to hold hands and wanted me laying on him, all while drying noticeable tears from my eyes. After the movies, we came home and he wanted to hang out with his homeboy. I was okay with it. It was hot and I did not want to be cooped up in no one's house on a Friday. I cut his hair not knowing this would be the last time I would run the Oyster clippers across his thick waves. We talked about how a person who was dying knew it was over. I chilled, watched television and he came in with a duffle bag and packed up his things. I got up and asked, "What's really going on?" He had nothing to say. As he packed, I helped. He left with a little struggle from me. I needed to know what happened between when he left to his jacked-up return. My mindset was my mouthpiece, "Oh, you got a job now and you're going to give me your ass to kiss. I thought we were cool?" He told me to allow him to leave and he was not cool when he left.

"So, who in your ear?"

"No one", he said. He did say he needed space and it was not about another woman. He called me on the Sunday before starting the job and he came over after I told him I needed a cigarette. Yes, I had started back smoking after years of quitting. He walked over and he expressed to me that he loved me and that we were still together but he felt we did not need to live together. I agreed. We made the best love and I said goodbye to him in the flesh for the last time before he left for Georgia. He did not have a phone so we made do with him using his friend's phone when he could. As the week went on he expressed again the importance of asking my friends and family for money because it would be a couple of weeks before he got paid. I listened and opened up to a few close friends and family that GOD laid on my heart. The first one was my cousin LaShawn. She told me to check my PayPal. I told each of my friends the truth and then I told them to give me what's in their hearts. My good friend Toi said to come to her. We were on E, making something out of what I had to eat. There wasn't a night that my family went hungry but the food was scarce. She rode with me to go get my granddaughter from daycare and she asked me about the grocery store I had told her about. We went to the good Giant Penny and she said to get you $40 worth of meat. I immediately thanked her and whipped my truck around and went to the store. On the way, out she handed me $160.00. I told her she will get it back. You have not because you ask not. My friend Honey, (Insider) told me to come to her house and get some money from her. What she handed me was fine but she asked me if I needed more, knowing I did but I said no. I was strapped for cash and at so many times and ways I have always been there for others. Now, I'm in need. I felt like I was about to lose my house, my mind, and my life. My peace was taken from me a long time ago.

I was living in hell in my own house and couldn't figure out what I did. I knew I was wrong. I didn't deserve to suffer like this. These are my true feelings. I wanted to know where his reaping was this change in my atmosphere. I had grown accustomed to feeling hurt, that it was normal to cry. I needed a change in my life and if I could get out of this interruption of everything, I would be back to testify the goodness of GOD and why it's important to be secure in my healing and deliverance. I was wrestling again in The Spirit and the flesh, knowing I had enough but the enemy wanted me to digest the fact that he had a job to do. However, I needed GOD to continue to take care of me like he started out in the beginning. That was not a part of my makeup and I could not venture out doing something I was not used to. It's hard letting go but the process of elimination was never easy.

Chapter 15

He started his out of town job and I was thankful for his blessing. I continued to hold on to a little bit of hope that things would get better and we could save this relationship. We didn't talk on the phone as much because again his phone was disconnected. I had to wait until he had the opportunity to use his friend's phone to have a conversation. Things were feeling like we were headed in a direction worth exploring until I looked at his Facebook page. I questioned him on the number of women he had as friends versus men. His response was all men wanted was women so he has more women on his page because that's all men talked about. I had the clueless look on my face because none of it made sense. However, my discerning powers had regulated the outcome. Here I was trying to do my work when I was supposed to leave this mess well enough alone. You know the old saying,

"A hard head makes a soft you know what". He knew I was uncomfortable with the situation. Not a bit insecure. Which he loved to say all the time. I felt respect was respect. Yeah, I know you're wondering or probably saying, how in the world are you asking for respect when you were with another woman's husband? Even though we were cordial and cool like that. I knew better. I own my truth and right my wrongs. It didn't dawn on me that his phone was back on because it's easy to connect to Wi-Fi and have access to your social media accounts. As Friday approached, I was still in my emotions about my direction and how I was going to get out of this foolishness that GOD was not pleased with. I received a text from him. So, I knew then his phone was back on. I asked him for some money. Here you are spending money, knowing I need some coins to handle business with bills.

We argued about that, to no avail. I hung up on him and he texts me these exact words, "My boss got my phone turned on. I have $1200 in my pocket and a raise. What you got?"

I immediately called back and said to him, "Are you gloating or are you thankful for what God is doing for you financially? You have money to spend and you know I need to handle some business and you're holding $1200 and you got a raise and not helping? You ran up bills too". He was quick to remind me this was my house and his name was not on anything. He then switched it up.

What he meant to say, "I already earned $1200 for the days I have worked so far. The boss man gave me a raise and turned my phone on. You know if I had some money I would send you some with no problem". Honestly, I did not believe that at all. He would have months ago but I knew then the lack of concern was another sign that it was over.

We had several conversations throughout the weekend but it was just talking. I prayed and even tried to improve how I responded and my tone. My love language was no longer loving and the woman I was turning into was not fit to sit on the throne as a queen. He was unsure when he would be back to the city because the job had him going hard. So, he said. He could have very well been back and I knew nothing about it. One thing I know, men tend to already have another woman set up when they walk out of your life, while you're still with them. Some desire to have a woman because they fear to be alone and many question their sexuality and want to prove to the world that they are not what others are thinking. It's a Monday morning in July and I'm feeling like a ton of bricks had hit me. I was not feeling myself as if I knew something was getting ready to shake my world. To satisfy me he sent me a friend request. I accepted and saw some subliminal post about our relationship. Like I said, I knew I wasn't happy so I knew he wasn't.

I looked through some post smiling at some of the spots he could capture on camera and came across a post he asked his followers, "What do I mean to you?" A female answered, "Your future. Like I said", with some emoji to give elaboration to what the future meant. She was from another state just like 85 percent of the other women on his page. Social media is not the downfall of a relationship. Whether they are out of order or in season. It's who operates the accounts that play the role in the demise. I did not feel threaten any whatsoever. I went to my page and posted one of my favorite pictures we'd taken at the beach, with the caption, "My favorite pic of us. love this man".

Later that evening without saying a word to what I had saw we talked and he wanted me to send him some pictures. He felt other men get pictures from their women and he wanted some from me. I felt like he didn't deserve to see me smile but I sent him a few anyway. When I went back to this page to see if he had posted any more pictures, I was blocked. I went outside on the front porch and called him. I asked him why he blocked me on Facebook.

His response was, "I didn't tell you to post any pictures of us on my page".

With a stunned face, I snapped back with, "Where is this coming from? We never had a problem posting our pictures".

He stated again as he was enjoying whatever it was in his mouth, "I did not tell you to post any pictures to of us on my page".

"First, dude I did not post the picture on your page I posted on my page and you saw it on the timeline. What do you have to hide? I see that's why you have all the out of state chicks on your page. So, when you go out of town you have no problem being who you say you are because they have no knowledge of me. That's why you are quick to holler no one is going to mess with you after being with me. Well, you know what you no longer have a woman". As soon as I said that, lightning struck across the sky and at the end of the bolt a shape of star formed. I hung up the phone and said thank YOU GOD! He was pleased with my actions and I immediately started crying. I put his calls on the block list and his text messages on spam.

I checked my messages the next day and noticed a call from him saying, "Stop being so mean. I love you. I want to talk to you". I was fumbling around with my phone and I realized that spam messages had its own folder. I checked it and the night of the last call, he had to text me goodnight as if nothing had happened. The next morning, I noticed he'd left this message.

"Have a great day". Again, as if nothing was wrong with the mess we were involved in. Because I had made up my mind I was done this time.

He sent another voicemail message with, "Hey baby I tried calling you all day. I love you I want to talk to you".

I kindly replied, "Leave me alone. I'm done".

His exchange to my decision was the most hurtful ending to my feeling for him, "I hate you".

He texts and later replies, "I love you".
"So, what you saying you don't want to be friends either".

"No, you have friends. Get with your out of state friends. I'm done. I'm not doing this any longer with you. You are not right for me and I'm not right for you. You're not worthy of me any longer. Your time is up". This is when my emotions started to twist and invited my stomach to a game of kickball.

"That's not fair", he said. "So why you hold me back so long to ruin my name? That's messed up. Lies you told your friend… but okay. I guess I will move on". There he was, again blaming me for something he clearly stated he was man enough to handle, along with the lies of being married and I suckered myself into the death of my own freaking mind, body, and soul with someone who turned out to be a stranger.

"How dare you come at me with this holding you back stuff? You knew what you were getting into with me. Lies I told who? I don't even talk to anyone you communicate with to even tell you anything I may have said. Reveal the friend. I have been faithful the hold time. You're the one who cheated".

"You are one mean individual. So, what I dabbled a little. I knew you were going to throw that in."
He then replies, "Your loss". Apparently, he's not recognizing the shifting in my atmosphere.

"No, my gain. I have suffered being in this relationship with you. You were my downfall and now I'm done with you".

"My feelings exactly when it comes to you. But no hard feelings. I still wish you the best. God bless you and I love you regardless". At this point, I felt like he wanted a reaction out of me and I was not willing to entertain him. I cried some more. I text and talked to my accountability partners. My sisters held me down during the times I needed them the most. As the week went on I'm struggling with how I was going to do this and pay that. By this time, I was out of bullets and Moses needed his gun back. My money is funny. My house is out of order. Why did I allow this to go on this long? I began to hear the amplified directive clearly, now that I had done what was pleasing to God's sight.

Chapter 16

I'm praying and praising GOD like I was at my last chance of getting it right. Yet, the devil still had a hold of what I truly had not let go of in my mind and heart and I began to sink into a depression. I didn't bathe unless I was going out. I didn't get out the bed some days because I had no life in me. If there wasn't a need for going anywhere, I laid my funky behind on the bed on sheets that needed washing. I had to go to Wal-Mart and GOD spoke to me. HE told me to be transparent and share my testimony. When I got home I got on Facebook where I share the inspirational post, quotes, memes, my "I Love the Chronicles Baby" videos and witty conversations to inspire women and girls through my truth.

I posted this, "I need my car insurance paid, my cable is about to get cut off, I don't have a gift for my granddaughter birthday tomorrow. I have borrowed, I don't steal. I still need my contacts, I pawned my TV. But I got me a bag of hair, glued those tracks in, executed my faith and let what was hindering me go. Challenged my faith to trust more, curse less, blame no one and hustle harder. I'm getting out of this hole. I see light". A few minutes after I followed up with this post.

"I was depressed, suicidal, stressed, angry, felt unworthy, lost trust, aggravated and I even wanted to give my house up, turn left out my driveway and salute to Charlotte. But God. You don't know what people are going through. You don't have an idea what she or he is dealing with behind closed doors. Yet, boss bitches and signifying monkeys with an untamed wig have the audacity to exist. Live Y'all. You don't know my story. But now you have a clue". I was a writing mess but GOD blessed it anyway. Within seconds, an anonymous inbox message asked me was I at home and I said I was. They told me they would come over in 10 minutes. Before they arrived, I received another call from a friend who did not want her name given that she appreciated everything that I do and have been a blessing to countless others and that she did not have much but she was going to bring what she had later after work. I'm overwhelmed with calls and text and inbox messages from complete strangers. One young lady said she only had $35 but she wanted me to have it. She came to my home and gave me a hug and I thanked her as well. The person that inbox me about coming in 10 minutes finally arrives. She comes in and gives me a big hug and let me know how much I have encouraged her and others. She said it wasn't much but she did what the Holy Spirit told her to do. She handed me an envelope with my name on it and told me to handle my business. I gave her a smile and a thank you and offered her to sit down. She said she didn't have time but she loves me and GOD bless and went on her way. I laid the envelope down and responded to someone else who wanted my account number to pay my car insurance. She sent the reply confirming her payment and told me to not let anyone know. She wanted to be anonymous as well too. When I went back to the envelope, enclosed were three crisps one hundred dollar bills enclosed. No, I was not expecting that amount but when **GOD** told me to testify and get transparent the overflow was a blessing and glory to HIS name.

Chapter 17

I'm finally single and detached from the unnecessary misery that we were both bringing on one another. We both wanted to be in love but we were in love with the wrong person. I knew what I needed and he even told me.

"DeVondia you need a man that is smart. A man that has money". I'm a firm believer that a man is to provide for his family. Call me old-fashioned if you want. I still see my dad do this for my mom. I can't accept anything less. When a man tells you what another man needs to have for you to be happy, take heed. This was the worst feeling in the world. When I stood out on the porch that breezy July evening, I had no idea that the relationship was going to dissolve. Tears came down my face more than the rain; which was needed to saturate the earth. Why was I crying? Why am I disappointed and feeling like I made a mistake? The purge became the enemy instead of the road towards my breakthrough. I wrestled with sleep and hardly ate. I kept my appearance up and wish I had taken summer classes. By doing so, I would have had something to occupy my idle mind. I decided I wanted and needed to go back to church. Pride, embarrassment, and guilt would not allow me to attend my home church. So, I solicited other churches for what I needed to feed my spiritual recklessness. I decided to attend a church not too far from my house.

When I arrived the first person I saw was a man who looked just liked him. He was a part of the parking lot ministry. You know, making sure members and guest park safely. I felt uneasy but I went inside. The Spirit was high and the word was rich and mighty. The man from the parking lot came inside when it was time for the church to end and when I looked at him again, I was amazed at how much he looked like my ex. The him that used to cut my grass, the man at the time was happily married to his wife, lawn service and driving trucks long distant. The man that had some business about himself and loved The LORD with his whole heart and didn't make excuses for going to church, because he wasn't ready. I left the church and when I got home I wanted to go sit with my neighbor. I called my daughter to bring me some flip flops from out of my room.

As she comes out the door, she burst out laughing. "Ma, is that him across the street?" I look out my rearview mirror and for the first time in my life, I had never been so scared. I wasn't afraid he was going to do something to me. I felt I was going to slip back into the abyss. I hurried up and ran into the house to use the bathroom. For some reason, I had a sudden urgency to go. When I got in the bathroom I ran water and cried out to GOD. I came back to the front of the house and my daughter was gone. I peeked out the blinds and saw him standing by an old white beat up car talking to my neighbor. I went back to the back of the house and called my neighbor and asked her if I could come down and talk to her. She was getting ready for a hot date but she said, "Come on". I left my car in the driveway and as soon as I saw him pull off I struck out running down the street in a pair of flip-flops. I was running for my life. I was running for my peace to not be interrupted. LORD, why is he in my neighborhood? Why won't he leave me well enough alone? As soon as I stepped foot onto my neighbor's porch he passes by. I'm shaking like a leaf in a breeze.

My neighbor looks at me and tells me, "DeVondia you are not over him. He has something on you. You need to free yourself from him". I knew that. My flesh didn't want to but my mind did. I talked to her until I got some comfort and until she was ready to leave for her date. I asked her to drop me off at home. When we pull up, he gets out the car and stands beside it as if he as trying to show off his come up. I guess he thought I was going to be impressed. No shade. Here I am scared to walk into my own house. As soon as I go in the house I peeped gently out the window and he blows the horn. I ignore it and opens a bottle of wine. My neighbor came back to sit with me after her date. I cooked some fish and we drank wine while we tried to figure out why we had the worst luck securing healthy relationships. I'm confused but I knew I needed to be alone. After she leaves, I got myself ready for bed. What begins to happen on this night was the power of GOD and GOD only. I took a hot shower and put lotion on. I felt the tears welling up in my eyes. I began to fight the tugging in my heart that was keeping me from being free of the struggle. LORD knows HE gave the ultimate sacrifice and this right here got me about to almost killed myself. Everything was strategically in its rightful place. Including, my girls being away from the house. I cried so much that my pillow was soaking wet. I don't know what had taken over me. Here I was crying and screaming and shortly after, a loud outburst. I felt as if another person was coming out of my body. I couldn't breathe. I struggled to embrace the process because it was uncomfortable and unfamiliar. Why is this happening to me? I didn't want to bother my cousin Ebony because she gets up early for work. I had just finished talking to my neighbor. I did not want to disturb her. But I needed somebody and I needed them now. I called Makeeba. I was harassed by my irregular breathing patterns. So, when I was telling her I was having a hard time, she thought I was saying I was having a heart attack. She talked to me until about 3:00 A. M. I can't remember ever I am crying like that. Makeeba said to me, "You are purging baby. Don't fight it". It hurt so bad to let go of a man that I loved so much., knowing good and well we were not healthy for one another. I needed GOD, I needed my house blessed, I wanted GOD, and I wanted my house anointed. I called Pastor Neal the next day and told him I needed him to come and anoint my house like he did when I got out the hospital in 2004. I did not expect him to say, "I will be there after I pick up Sister Neal.

We will be right on". I cleaned up my house and something said clean under your bed. I ran the broom under the bed and a pair of his shoes appeared. I took the shoes and some other items he left behind and put it outside in the trash can. When I went back out, later, to throw something else away, I noticed the shoes looking as if it were walking out of the trash can. I know I threw the shoes in the trash can. Why were these shoes looking as if it was getting ready to come up out of that trash can, side by side, left on the left and the right on the right? I shook it off and didn't pay it any mind. But I did bring it my accountability sisters attention. It's important to have ladies you can trust and that will be responsible for being accountable to you. I tell people, I don't hang with a big crowd but I have a team of bad chicks that will drop what they're doing and pray for me, pray with me and put me in my place. Too many have friends that are condoning what their friends are doing and no one is responsible for the other. So, the whole crew is failing. But they slay…So they say. I did not want to call my Pastor and First Lady because I was embarrassed. I called my sisters that I felt had the strength I needed when I was down and strong enough to build me up when I saw no way out. LaShawn Walls, Candice Watts Greene, Makeeba Jackson, thank you for your selfless acts, and Teresa Legrand for coming in your sheriff's uniform from work. Pastor Neal and First Lady Neal anointed me, the ladies, and prayed a prayer that was not only for me but it also uplifted the ladies. That night was the best night's sleep I had in a long time. I guess those shoes were keeping me awake at night.

Chapter 18

With everything that was going on in my life, I was not allowing anything or anyone to come to my academic excellence. If only I took that much responsibility for my personal life, things would be oh, so sweet. Football season had kicked off and it was time for jerseys and jeans, freshly waxed brows and a hairdo to match my new attitude. I was finally free. I used my refund checks from school to help subsidize my income. GOD has never forsaken me, never. Even when I had no food he made sure I ate. When I needed a bill paid he made sure it was covered. Why couldn't I be like that towards myself? I pour out and deposit into so many without wanting anything in return. Yet, my strength needed replenishing. My faith was always tested. HE gives HIS hardest test to the ones HE knows can and will endure till the end. Even those who make a fool out of themselves. I know there's a magnificent peace waiting to smother me like rice and gravy. I was taking more selfies and standing in front of my full body mirror; noticing the dramatic weight loss. I was not working out nor had I changed up my diet. Fall had finally invested its foliage in the trees and the unseasonable like the weather was perfect for cracked windows and a low-speed ceiling fan. One day, I am sitting in my living room scrolling through my timeline and I noticed a picture of one of my friends that made me look twice. I complimented him and we began a friendship that happened on purpose but ended abruptly. Fast forward a little, because I don't want to spend too much time on it but I felt this part was necessary. I had been struggling with whether I should continue advocating for HIV and sharing my story. Truth be told I was burnt out. We will call him temporary. Because it did not last but a minute. He told me I was a good girl and he liked me a lot. But the only hang up he had was, I had not let go of my past.

"If GOD has done what you said HE has done for you, leave it alone and quit talking about it".

I start running around the yard. I finally got my confirmation. I made the December 1, 2015, my last speaking engagement. It was time for me to tap into my other gifts and talents that GOD has blessed me with. I was working on my Bachelor of Arts in communication and discovering more about who I was through the college experience; than any other time in my life. Well, my temporary and chill lasted for about a month and then it was on to what a single girl does best. I was doing me. One late October day in 2015, I decided to wash that gray right out of my hair. After I applied my dye, there was a knock at the door.

After asking who it was, I was surprised to hear the voice that asked, "Does Vonda still live here?" We will call him Throwback. Throwback was a guy I knew from back in the day. We had a crazy chemistry. We laughed together well, we joked a lot and acted like Pam and Martin but our bodies fit like a hand in glove when we were together. We had a conversation that allowed us to catch up since 20-years ago. My evening's drop by and chill, turned into me putting on clothes and going out. I felt connected all over again with him. Long story short, I don't want to spend too much time on Throwback either, but it's necessary. He was living with a woman that he made claims, was not all that. So, my mindset was, I've been tried before. What you're not going to do is play me. I found myself stretching myself thin, between spending time with him, classes and gearing up for winter break and my speaking engagement. I was excited about this being my final curtain. For 10-years I had been sharing and advocating, teaching and praying. Now my time was up. As people began to fill the seats in Biddle Hall at Johnson C Smith University, I sat quietly on the front row, the right of the stage. I look to my left and asked my oldest daughter was that my ex.

She burst out laughing, "Yes". She tells my granddaughter, Zion, "There goes Paw Paw". She cried to go sit with him. I was mad that she wanted to. I was even more mad that he had shown up.

What does he want? After I did my thing on stage and hugging and taking pictures with my supporters; my best friend Tiffany says to me, "Um Miss. Roseborough, this gentleman here would like to take a picture with you". I took the picture. You should have seen my face. You should have seen him cheesing like a Cheshire. He sent me a message on my author business page letting me know that he was proud of me and that it was good to see me again. He was proud of me and that he was missing me. LORD knows I was missing him too. Throwback didn't open doors and I would stand outside the car until he opened it and would talk junk while he did it. I would laugh and shake my head. It was the little things that a gentleman does that had me comparing my ex to what was before me. During this time, I was smoking and it was taking a toll on my body. I wanted to stop but I was at ease when I inhaled and exhaled. I was on a mission.

I and Throwback looked good together, we felt good together and we even gave them fever during the winter in fall like weather. His words were, "You took me from that woman". I sure did. You might as well be where you're happy. Why did I do that? It was good for about two weeks. My transmission went out in my truck and he allowed me to use his to get back and forth. I knew I was going to get me something when my coins came. But I had not made up my mind to what kind of car I wanted. I receive an alert on my phone form someone that sent me a video of my ex-polishing a woman's toes. I felt some type of way because he was confessing his love for me but pushing another woman's cuticles back. I hid the fact that it hurt but I had a rebound that was keeping me occupied. I'm still not going to church. However, I'm praying for better days. I start feeling like the chemistry between Throwback and I was fizzling out. After my Panthers devastating loss in the Big Game, I started thinking that what we were doing was a waste of time. I got my new car and then I got brand new. I didn't want him to think because I got my car I no longer needed him. I didn't. He was feeling the same way but wasn't man enough to share this with me. He went his way and I went mine. I thought back on the day I cried on my mama's lap about my situation with my ex. She told me if it's meant to be it will come back around.

Chapter 19

I was finally living the single life. No worries on whether he was pulling another stunt or if I was going to be pissed off at him for not having enough of money for me to spend. Now, our relationship was not one-sided. I will own my faults and intelligence I had in this relationship.

As he would say, "This is your house, the bills are in your name. Ain't nothing in here belong to me". Yet, the accumulation of watts determined that enough people lived in my house. With, provide, so Duke Energy can get the share we owe. I missed him. My ex that is. I received a call from the hardworking man. He wanted me to meet him at his job. I told him about what had been going on with me.

His words were, "Stop moving them negroes in your house that can't do nothing for you. Go home and pack some clothes. Meet me at my house or beat me there. I get off at 5:00". I wasn't going down there. I didn't need any extra in my life. He told me he had a refrigerator, furniture, and his own kitchen table. I knew what he was saying but I knew I wasn't ready to be booed up with anyone else. I still missed my ex. It's right before Valentine's Day 2016 and I'm excited about life. However, someone was missing. I inbox my ex on Facebook from my author page. That's how we communicated.

We were secretly having; You hurt me, you were wrong, I'm sorry, and I forgive your conversations there. I messaged him, "I miss you…come home". For two weeks, I did not hear anything from him. Then, I received an alert with an apology for not checking his messages sooner.

We shared hours of conversation before he said, "Come get me". Here I go again. Going back to the very thing that had me bound. I loved him. Did I love him or was it a soul tie? I asked him about the lady he was with and the story was; work was short and they had to move from the hotel they were living in back to his relative's house.

"So, are you going to leave her there?" He had a funny way of not putting an end to what did not matter in his life. He's a gentle man with a kind heart. You know the one that doesn't like to burn bridges, just in case they must cross it again. This irked me. My thing is, let her know what the business is so she will not be thinking there's hope. She called several times until he finally got the nerve to let her know that he was with someone else now and she had 2-weeks to find herself somewhere else to live. On several occasions, I witnessed her crying over the phone, asking why he was doing this to her. Then in the last round, he was informed to BLOCK her. I'm feeling high and mighty now. I get what I want. He's a good man and why is he living any kind of way out here.

We all knew the difference in him from when he was with me and when we were apart. I did my best to make him happy but my best wasn't enough. The woman he wanted was the woman I was in my first book. I told him to be careful what he asked for. That woman was dead. I'm no longer the woman that the women hated and the men yearned to love. I was a changed woman unchained from my past ways and I was looking forward to a rich future with him. Even though he came back the same way he left, lying. Oh, he had the papers for the divorce done and he was going off to school to get back what the devil stole from him. All I kept hearing was how much I deserved to get the best and have the world. Empty promises, like the ones I made when I would promise him good loving. To be honest, I was tired. I had my hay day and I wasn't into sex like I used to be. See, when I asked GOD years ago to numb me from my belly button down, HE did that. I wanted to be married, I didn't want to be out here doing just anybody. Even though I wasn't going to church, I still had the word in my heart. I was convicted on so many levels and at times I would still hear GOD. I told him these words, "We are not having sex until you get the divorce. I can sleep in the bed with you and not have sex with you. I have power and control. If you can't do this, then you may need to move on". He wanted to do whatever made me happy. He took out the trash, cooked full course meals, washed the car, clothed and even dropped me off and picked me up from school.

He had me extra spoiled and I loved it. He found ways to make money until work picked back up. This was the test of our relationship because soon he was going off to Boston to work and would be gone for 2-weeks. Prior to him leaving, he helped me with my annual fish fry. People loved seeing us together. We made love look good and for a while, it was like us being together for the very first time. We gave each other the best that we had. I stuck to my guns and didn't pull them out the holster.

I meant what I said, "No sex". I loved how he called my name, DeVondia.

I loved when he would say, "DeVondia I'm going to marry you. You will be my wife". This excited me. I was ready to be Mrs. I was ready for the red, white and black formal event that would bridge the union between two people and make us one. I was eager to plan, prepare, try on dresses and pick my bridesmaids. All of what I was thinking about had a price tag attached to it. Instead of looking like a goal digger I was looking like I was trying to do too much with so little. This is my first wedding and my budget was not extreme. The covenant is what is most important. I wanted to stay together after the wedding ceremony. All I had to do was keep reminding myself that the mortgage was due, right after the date he set. He oversaw setting the date and I didn't mind at all.

Chapter 20

Inquiring minds wanted to know the wedding date. I would always direct them to the one that had the task of deciding it. One day he slickly promoted the date on my Facebook page. I was excited. October 8, 2017. My birthday. I was going to be the future Mrs., on my 46th birthday. Now, I need a ring. Everything was backward; he was still married and I was engaged to a separated man. I was given a wedding date before the ring. Lord, have mercy. Help this mess. I was good while we were apart. The 2-week work trip to Boston turned out to be a month. Absence makes the heart grow fonder. I missed him. We video chat, we text, and we talked until it was time to pick him up from the airport. Things were still good. No cares and no worries. We continued to dream out loud and make plans for our future. Here it was late June and I had less than a week left of summer classes. He had another job assignment that was taking him an hour and some change away. We both felt it would be a great getaway for the both of us. He talked to his boss man and he said it was okay, since all the guys had their own rooms, the rest of the fellas followed suit and brought their families along too. For the entire month of July, we drove down to Columbia South Carolina on Monday mornings and was headed back no later than 9:00 AM on Fridays. We basically, came home to wash clothes to pack for the next week.

When he got his first check I told him it was necessary to get this divorce finalized. I got a number from my cousin for a divorce lawyer and his secretary emailed the papers and we went to the nearest Office Max and printed it off. We couldn't do anything else until we returned to Charlotte. I was happy that he was taking the initiative to get this done. I was tired of living the way we were. I probably held out from having sex with him for about a month. My mindset was if I don't someone else will. We must remind ourselves that we are worth waiting for and if he's not willing, he is not worth the time. I started telling myself, he will be my husband and he was getting the divorce. Don't ever negotiate sin while trying to justify why it's not wrong. Sin feels good. The opportunity that was before me was not like no other. What other man has done the things he has done for me? No one. I finally got my just due. We were on our way back to Charlotte and our first stop was the Wells Fargo to get the papers notarized and for him to get the money order and mail it off to the lawyer. The bank representative that sat down with us shared her story about her husband being married when they met and what they had to go through to get their divorce. Just because someone shared with you their story doesn't make it your testimony. He got the money order and we were both excited about getting the paperwork back. Now, can I please get a ring to set this thing off, right? We didn't have a lot of money and I'm not a flashy kind of women but I do know how to dress nicely within my means.

I can make the expensive stuff look like mine cost some change too. I know how to wear clothes, coordinate, and accessorize. Many didn't even know that I was recycling what I had and made it look brand new. While I was in Columbia, he sent me shopping to buy some sundresses and a purse. While he was at work, I stayed in the room writing and working on my clients' books until he got off. Once he showered, we would go out to eat and explore the city. Once the assignment was over we were back home for good. During this time, I hated coming home. I did not feel the peace that I desired. Both my daughters and my granddaughter were living with us and I was ready for the nest to be empty. They both got their assigned eviction month and date, January 15. I wanted us to enjoy the house for once as a couple, alone.

Chapter 21

I knew everyone was not happy about us being back together. I could tell. Even with some of our own family members. Those that used to love on me barely even spoke and a few of mine didn't come around. But we were in it for one another. We did not care what anybody thought. Whether it was Facebook or family. We were grown and we knew we had feelings for each other. So, for those of you that took the time to not hug me, kiss my jaws and even speak when I came around, I still love you. That's the only way to be. Agape.

Pause for the Cause...

Single women should never feel as if they must have a man. Every woman is not going to get married and every woman is not going to get a divorce. You must make up in your mind that you're worth waiting for. During this wait, here are some tips to make this process one that doesn't make you feel as if you're locked up while waiting on Mr. Right to release you from everything that has you bound. For those of you that follow me on Facebook, you may remember this post. In preparation for waiting on your man; I have done it and see others state the word, Wait.

I looked the word 'Wait' up and this was the definition that stuck out to me, "To remain inactive or in a state of repose, as until something expected happens (often followed by for, till, or until) to wait for the bus to arrive." We cannot wait till a man arrives, we must be in an active state of prayer, fasting, and preparation. Praying for you first and foremost to be the woman of GOD to the man of GOD that GOD is preparing for you or has prepared for you but you have not because you are waiting instead of preparing yourself. Prepare your home by anointing EVERYTHING, bless it accordingly and keeping it clean. Making sure that your home runs in a way that you forget you're single because you're in a wife state of mind. Fasting for the deliverance of things and people that have a strong hold on your mind, body, and soul.

So that you're FREE of the unexpected visitors waiting to distract you. Waiting on a man should not be like waiting for a bus because an accident can happen, a detour can take the route off course, and it can have mechanical problems. Prayer is essential but also stay busy so that you are conquering your goals. You're not only preparing to be a prepared wife but a successful one. Just my thoughts.

Chapter 22

The assignment in Columbia SC had ended and I was back to, I wish we could go somewhere state of mind. Things were okay, but not like what people thought when they saw us on the street or what we posted on Facebook. I was drained. I had the feeling of a Libra. My scales were unbalanced and I knew why. I was spiritually broken, living in sin and not trying to be bothered at times. Depression would slip in on me like a thief in the night and I would have every cause to curse anybody out that was not in order. I needed peace, not broken promises. The boss man had not paid him all his money for the work that he had done but we made what he gave him to do until then. I was ready for a ring. The first ring he got me, he put it on lay-a-way at a pawn shop. I was okay with it. I was there. I helped pick it out. The second ring he got me I picked it out as well and got it from the Wal-Mart. It wasn't anything big and blinging. I am not the big and blinging type. I don't feel any type of way about where the ring came from. I would do it again and the next time, with the right man. He put it in lay-a-way and I was the happiest girl on the planet. All I knew was, he was paying for it and he made sure I didn't know about it. I promised him more of me once the divorce was final. I couldn't and wouldn't do certain things with him or to him because he was still married. I know someone is saying, you were already in there, you should have gone for the gusto. Well, I didn't. It was still an amazing bunch of mercy and grace upon me and daily, I stretched my arms to The LORD for a sign. He said I was spoiled. I told him it was his fault. He said I was evil. I told him he made me that way. He called me a bitch. I called him a punk ass bitch. The respect factor continued to go out the window and we were now a basic couple. It was nothing extraordinary about our love anymore. The luster was gone. The I'm in love, I love him were lies. I was glowing in those pictures I posted because I was happy with continuing my education and being on the campus of my HBCU is where I found my peace. I wanted the cable off for some reason. As I type this I recognize it was preparation season for the transition that was getting ready to occur. Before that, I found the reason why I fell in love with him. We were all over one another once again and it was feeling good. The work was slow, but he was offered another job at the airport. In the meantime, I was busy planning our red, black and silver engagement slash my birthday party with close family and friends. My beautiful bridesmaids showed up but one. The one that had been knowing me for the longest, said my brother would be down with the balloons and beer and of course she could not make it due to an unforeseen situation. Well, it's the following year and I have yet to see those items. She came by a week later to invite us to dinner. I was already cooking and he was at work. I let her tell her story and then I told her how I felt. When I broke down in tears that's when she said what she has been feeling all along, "See how it feels when you didn't show up for granddaddy?" Her granddaddy didn't know that I did not show up for his funeral. Not trying to sound insensitive nor abrasive but her grandfather passing was the hardest thing next to losing my grandmother. I just couldn't do it and she did not understand that. So, you want to play tick for tac. I told her to get the hell out of my house and she didn't have to ever worry about me again. Of course, she said, "I would have never said that to you". She's not me. I was mad as hell. Life went on and we had a marvelous time. My bridesmaids and family were there and we played music, a few games while he and the men were outside. He felt left out because I and the girls were playing games and he was outside cooking. I made it all about me. I was very selfish, I will admit that. He did everything possible to make sure I enjoyed that day. A beautiful cake from my daughter, drinks, gifts and good food prepared by my mom and sister. Besides me being selfish, and my long-time best friend not holding her corner, I think the engagement party was a flop. Nothing was what I expected it to be. I didn't get the kneel and will you marry me proposal. When he got the ring, I didn't know. I was cooking breakfast and he was already telling me I needed to tighten up before he put it on my finger. But he put it on my finger anyway.

Chapter 23

You would have thought I was excited about everything falling into place; well sometimes I was and other times I wish I had thought this thing through. Apart from me wanted to marry him and the other parts of me didn't want to waste his time. I had fallen out of love with the very man, I felt **GOD** had sent to me. The divorce papers were filed and he received the documents acknowledging that he was indeed divorced from her, two days after my birthday and our engagement party. That there alone was the clear sign that I did not pay attention to. That's why my party didn't go as planned. Now truth be told, I had a nasty attitude with this man. The wickedness that was within me sometimes scared me. He called me evil and I would curse him out for things I felt as a man, he should've known. I will be honest, I know I did not make him happy and he tried his best to make me smile; knowing good well I was not worth it. I took advantage of his kindness at times. I took advantage of his passive-aggressive demeanor and it felt good. Until I realized that I didn't need a man that I could control. He would say I was happier when we had money. He was correct. As soon as payday rolled around I had a pep in my step and I was ready to go cash his check. He made me feel I was obligated for this moment. Whether it was every week or every other week, I was down for my palms being greased with crispy one hundred dollar bills. Even though I spent the money on bills, he knew I wasn't a powder head, spending stupidly, eating out and buying clothes and shoes trying to impress people or making someone else rich. If you continue to tell me I deserve it all and you gave your all to the wrong person, then yes, I want what you think rightfully belongs to me. I felt neglected in the. My point was always valid, you're my man, you turn a key, you use water, lights, and enjoy watching cable, so what he was talking about didn't bother me at all. Because I still got the money. I had to remember that I was keeping house before him and I didn't mind doing it again. I went to bed with pajama pants on and a nightgown. I had lost interest in having sex. Now, the sex was great. However, when the chemistry was no longer there, the drought made its appearance. Making promises to do whatever with him or to him when I got out of school or when my homework was complete and I still neglected him. I was not ready to be in the company and companionship of a man for the rest of my life. There you go, I said it. I was not ready. Why? Because I deserved so much more. I didn't need a man that was jealous of me, who had an opinion on the number of Facebook friends I had and that I was getting more likes on my page than he was. Self-esteem was an issue for him. He has been through a lot in his life and he spoke to me about some personal things that would make you want to put your hands on some folks. One thing I know from experience until you let go of your past, you cannot effectively move forward.

I asked him many times to seek to counsel and he shot me down. I tried to coach him from a life coach standpoint but he said time and time again that he did not want to be one of my patients. I told him, I don't have patients, I serve clients. His issues were bigger than me and I know when to stay in my lane. I was not trying to diagnose, prescribe, or write a doctor's note for something I did not understand myself. I had to force myself to be cordial with him in the home. He switched his job at the airport to be a cashier at the neighborhood store, I supported his decision and shook my head at the same time. The money was good, paid weekly but the hours were very long. I'm a full-time student so it was easy for me to go down to the store and sit with him when he was there alone. I felt iffy about some things but I kept it to myself. Before I get into that, let me talk about the people he befriended in the neighborhood. I'm like this, I don't sit up in people's houses and I don't want people sitting up in mine. I speak and mind my business. Now if you need me to help you with something or an ear, I'm the person to come to. I have been a loner all my life. People don't believe me when I tell them how many siblings I have. You don't see a lot of foot traffic in and out of my house unless it's fish fry season and that's pretty much how I like it. It's a select few that come through and take their shoes off and recline back and break bread with me. So, when he connected with the neighbors, I reminded him of that. It was nothing against anyone, it's just a cultural thing.

The way I was raised. He connected with a couple and they seemed sweet. I never knew them by name, but I would sometimes speak. I was some timey like that. However, when he moved in with me, he was the welcome committee. I didn't mind. I was glad that he was being more social. I had tons of homework to do and he had some entertainment when I couldn't cater to his needs. Him going across the street became excessive to me at times but it was what it was. For the moment, it's what the guys did; drink their beer, tell lies and every now and then, support each other with a hi-five. He got excited when I told him I was going to come over with him one day and sit with them. Finally, I grabbed my yard chair, whatever I was drinking at the time and we went to be neighborly. The young lady of the house was honored to have my company and I admit I had some good times and laughs with them. We became a unit. We would cookout and serve them and they reciprocated. When he went to the store to get his elixir, at times he looked out for them. I would slowly hibernate back into my house and get on the laptop. There was always a chapter for me to complete, an assignment to start, or I simply wanted to be alone. We would invite them to come out to eat crab legs with us or share opportunities for us to engage in grownup activities together but it never manifested. I got so comfortable with them that I began to share our issues. Sometimes she and I would go off to the side and have a conversation about our men. He had stressed me out so bad at the beginning of our relationship I had started back smoking cigarettes. I remember my sister-friend Toi Parks telling me, if she had not seen me fire a cigarette up, she wouldn't have known because I never smelled liked most people do, that smoke. I was discreet about what I did and who I did it around. I even started back smoking weed. Oh, he loved that, but I knew there was something else I could be doing with my money. I'm rolling joints the long way but feeling some type of way because I wasn't happy at all. I cried myself a headache because I didn't want to hurt him. But that pull on that cigarette and after inhaling that joint took me back to that place and suddenly; I was back in love again.

Chapter 24

I wish I had kept my damn car. My Hyundai Sonata had all the bells and whistles. But that flyer kept coming in the mail from the Hyundai dealership about upgrading to a new one. We knew it would be a great opportunity to get a new car with a warranty and a few other perks that made me smile. But when that dealer took us to an all-white, Hyundai Accent, I began having second thoughts. I haven't been more unsure about getting that car than anything I've ever done in my entire life. How in the world do you get a car with a man that you find yourself sometimes in love with? He knew I didn't like the car. He said I could keep my car and he would take over the payments for the new car. I sure wish I had taken him up on that. Let me talk about me for a chapter. I found myself not easy to love. At times, I didn't want him to love me so much because I knew it was going to be a day that I was going to fold. Let's start with my past relationships. Every committed relationship that I've been in, I was the one that was taking care of the man. Before my ex-fiancé, I never had a man to take care of the things, that he did. Very early in the relationship, I was spoiled. You know the person that act like they never had anything before? Well, I wasn't that person because I was a kept woman before him. However, the gifts he showered me with and the money he splurged on me, the cleaning and washing, fixing things around the house, taking out the trash, washing the car, always kept the gas tank on tilt, was a bonus to the dream I always had the man that would eventually sweep me off my feet and take good care of me. I was not raised by my biological father and he didn't share a major role in my life. Like I said in my first book, Put it on Paper, he didn't show me how a man was supposed to treat a lady. I was again in love with the wrong person. He was my illusion, pieces of him would certainly help build a man fit for a queen. I was desperate to be in love and finally, someone had popped the question and wanted me to be his wife for the life. But DeVondia still had baggage. I was disgusted by a disease that I didn't want to interfere with my love life. Would he truly be able to stand by my side if I got sick? Would he be responsible for my well-being? Could he handle the public's stigma that could oppress him into going left, when he promised me right here is where he would stay? These questioned barricaded my mind and made me angry at myself for allowing it to happen in the first place. Then I would start an argument to test his staying power. There were times when he knew what I was doing and there were many more times when he told me I was pushing him away. He would do anything for me and I knew that. Did I take advantage of that? No, I did not. I was well within my rights to have doors opened for me, chairs pulled out for me, bills paid and the utmost respect. At times, I didn't show him how much I appreciated him. I didn't.

I promise you I'm being honest. Being a head-strong, fearless, alpha female; who never had a loss for words and sometimes he couldn't handle the animation that came with me. I have a voice of a storyteller and it sounded like a mystery and other times I was as ugly as a horror story. Whatever the tone, it was always something that I promised to work on. My mouth was so nasty towards him. I didn't deserve a man. I was too selfish and self-centered at times. I was a spoiled brat and I needed a strong man that could handle me and to let me be me but have a sincere approach to comforting my attitude. However, I needed to check myself. I woke up many mornings on the wrong side of the bed. I kept my legs closed with that man more than I did when I didn't have one. I already wrote about my past. So, don't expect to hear about it in depth here. I wasn't ready because I was still healing from all the other stuff before him. I was a reasonable person. Except, I hogged the remote control. We had no love for the same television shows. I was into reality shows, comedies, and drama. He was Sci-Fi and Naked and Afraid. I was into sports all day and night, he wasn't. I would compromise and bring myself into his world and he would do the same. We just couldn't agree to disagree. It was always an argument. I was a hot mess in love one minute out of love the next. I was hopeful at times that my mind and body would line up with his needs. Then I felt it would be okay if we broke up, I would be alright. Was I prepared to be alone?

Was I ready to be single again? I asked myself these questions many times. I couldn't imagine my life without him but I could imagine me being without him. He was a great friend and trust me we both deserved that. He seemed happier working at the neighborhood store. He had a lot of responsibility; including, opening and locking up. That meant the times I was used to sharing with him had dwindled down so bad, that when he got off work I was ready to go the bed. It was taking a toll on our already strained relationship. He wanted me to spend time with him at the store and since it was time for winter break, I would go down and spend hours with him. The store owner didn't like it of course. So, I had to back off. But it didn't stop me from going down there to see my man. Things got so hectic one day that he called me stressed the hell out about wanting to quit. I was on his last nerve and the job was so stressful but he asked me to come down while he locked up the store and dropped the keys in the drop box. Again, I supported him. It was right before the Christmas holiday and it was almost time for the second car payment. The tension was so thick you could cut it with a knife. But I told him to get some rest and chill. He made promises that he couldn't keep, just like I did. We were now in a financial bind and I had to pull the extra weight. That's what a woman is supposed to do right? I was being selfish again. When was it going to be my turn to spend my money my way and not having to bail a man out?

I did it to myself. I should have kept my car.

Chapter 25

It was Christmas Eve and his sister had called to see if we all could get together for lunch. That entire day he and I argued over stupid stuff. I decided to go out and UBER for a little while but found it was rather slow so I headed down the service road towards my house. Halfway down the road, I called to let him know that his sister had called and confirmed our outing for the day. No answer. I called again, the same thing. When I pulled up he was standing off from his friends talking to a woman that I recognized but didn't know who she was.

So, I pull up to the curb and pull the emergency brake and park, hollering out, "So you over here in this bitch face but can't answer your phone". I'm pissed. What you're not going to do is play me and I know about it. I get out the car and start walking towards them. My neighbor was standing off to the right of them, looking confused. My neighbor had witnessed me get out of character with my ex-plenty of times. I lost all respect for him and myself. I've thrown his clothes out on the lawn, I've talked about his manhood and cursed him from here to South Africa but he still loved me. I wanted to be the one to break up with him but turn around and beg him to stay. I didn't want to be alone. I decided that if I can't have what I deserve, then I will take what I can get. As I became more bitches, he became more punks. We would apologize and act like we were in love all over again. He would wine me and dine me but underneath all that foolishness I wanted out. By this time, I'm so upset with him in this woman face I repeated myself again.

"So, this why you can't answer the phone because you're over here in this bitch face. Don't play with me". He is looking confused at this point and then my neighbor comes over stuttering like hell, telling me it's not like that and then she opens her mouth.

"Ma'am it ain't like that".

"Bitch I'm not talking to you. I'm talking to my man and you have 3.5 seconds to get your ass across the street".

I walked off, got in my car and by the time I parked my car he had made his way towards me. Hugging up all on me trying to convince me I'm the only one. I looked at him believing nothing he said. His sister was on her way and when she arrived we loaded up in her truck and went off to eat. The entire time she was talking about not allowing him to go to his grandfather's house where their mother lived. The grandfather was a rootworker and she insisted that since she left home, life has been better for her and she had no intentions of going back.

Her exact words were, "If you want to keep money in your pocket and for your car to keep running, do not go over there and keep him from over there". How was I going to keep that man away from his family? Especially, his mother.

I was all in, asking questions and feeling some type of way. I asked her if her mother practiced roots. She just gave me a funny look. I told her that their mom gave him a bag of potatoes to bring to the house and all she said was, "You better get it out your house". One the way home, I sat in the back seat while he sat up front with his sister trying to explain our issues to her. My point was, whatever you share, make sure you tell where you fucked up. The evening was drawing near and his sister had voiced many times that she was headed home. Before we knew it, it was Christmas morning. Early that morning he woke up and went to go share some sibling time with her in the living room. I got up and told him to come to me. I felt it was only right to initiate some holiday nookie.

After loving on one another for a minute and asking him for what would be the last time, "Do you want to go to church with me this morning?"

"Nah babe, I will get the dinner ready". I always called him a heathen after he would deny my request. Church hurt had scorned him so bad that he didn't want to be bothered with the likes of any ministry. I wanted to know where my youngest daughter was. She told me that she would go to church with me on Christmas morning, but for some reason, it was a ghost town. His sister came into my room and told me that she would go with me but she wasn't invited. I told her she was more than welcome to go to church with me. My hot water heater was busted. It began with a leak

THE AWAKENING OF DEE

that was seeping from the closet where the hot water heater was, through my bedroom closet, under my wood flooring. We were putting towels down daily and washing towels two times a day. Some days it wasn't as bad as the others. However, we had to boil water to take baths. I would use the biggest pots I had, filled the pots up with water, and turn my stove on high to make the perfect tub of bath water. He promised to get it fixed and every time I got my hands on some money a bill needed to be paid. I didn't invite people over because I was embarrassed. I didn't want anyone to know. The ones that did, only one person offered to assist, and that was my best friend Tiffany. I wasn't expecting anyone to help us out. I had a man living with me that had just quit his job because he was stressed the hell out. Well, I was too. His sister and I got ourselves together and headed out the door to my church. Church was good and all I can remember was it was time for a change. After church, I'm one that goes down to speak to my Pastor and First Lady. I went to my First Lady, exchanged pleasantries and then headed back to the pew where I left his sister.

When I got back in her presence she said to me, "Let me find out you are one of the ones that hang around after church".

I replied with a simple, "I fellowship. Come on lets' go down and speak to my Pastor and then we can leave". When I walked down towards my Pastor, he asked me who was this I had with me; I introduced her as his sister. Her greeting was not at all warm and I saw the Holy Spirit push my Pastor back and the two didn't make any contact whatsoever. Right then is when I started paying attention to the signs. Everything I ignored started funneling around in my mind, like a category five storm.

Chapter 26

Before I got out the church's parking lot good, I had spewed out a few hardcore curse words. When I made the left turn onto my street, he was getting ready to cross the street holding a beer in hand. He stopped in the middle of the street and started dancing in front of my car. I rolled the window down and this is how it went.

"Where are you going?"

"I'm just going across the street and chill for a little bit. He gave me a beer".

"It's Christmas. You have family here just like they do. Let them have their time and you need to come on and be with your family.

"Babe, I washed the dishes and prepared the turkey, I just left out of the house checking on it". I don't know what came over me but here is when things got real. The language is getting ready to change. The rage is coming from a place where I couldn't even identify who I was and here is when I made the best decision in my life. He went across the street for a minute and came right back. I quickly noticed the Georgia tag on a car that belonged to the woman I confronted him about the day before. He was talking to his sister and I overheard him telling her how things were between me and him.

I came outside and hollered out, "If you going to tell it, make sure you tell it all. Tell her how you call me bitches and I clap back and say your mama". At this point, I am .38 hot and .45 cocked. I'm coming from a place that I wasn't familiar with. The rage came from a pit within that was red like fire and my immediate defense was to defend me. His sister was saying whatever she was saying to him and looking like the devil she said the Pastor at her old church said she was before he put her out.

I hollered out "Fuck Y'all" on Christmas Day to him and her. I went back in the house and he was hollering, "See what I mean?" I began to feel bad. So, I went outside to apologize to his sister.

She said to me, "I'm scared of you. I'm not coming over there".

"Well get the fuck from in front of my house". One of the neighbors from across the street came over and I told him to take his ass back where he lived.

He went on. I grabbed the keys to the car and I pulled up beside her jeep and said, "Get your shit and get the fuck out and take his motherfucking ass with you".

She replied, "What happened?"

"She put me out sis. Let me get my stuff". I took a ride to cool off. Like any other time, I felt like it was just a disagreement but when I pulled into the driveway he was hauling his belongings out the house; telling the neighbors to standby as witnesses. I went in the house and pulled the gun out of the draw. With everything in me, I still have no idea what was happening to me. He asked me if I was going to kill him now. He told me this was it, you said for the last time to get out and I'm leaving.

"Get the fuck on then", I said. I grabbed him by his arm and he pushed me, I fell against the bedroom door and slipped on something wet on the floor. I heard him telling the people outside, she slipped and fell and trying to act like something is wrong with her.

He came back inside to gather some more items and stepped over me and said, "I'm out of your hair bitch". I got up and took the ring off my finger and placed it in his hand.

He went out the door and went his merry way. I took to Facebook and wrote, "The wedding is off!" My play mama, Tina Elder Way called me on the phone and I was hysterical. She said, "I'm on my way". When she arrived, I cried on her shoulder and she told me to get it out. I told her everything.

The first thing she asked me was, "Give me the bag of potatoes and do you have some sage?" I did. She put some in a pot and boiled it and explained that anything negative must flee out of your house right now. She began to pray and opened the door for anything that was on me to get on. I didn't feel like myself for a while. I wasn't happy, I was always angry, and would jump down his throat quick. Like I said many times before, I hated when he was home but missed him when he was gone. I prayed and I cried and cried and prayed until the feeling left me. It was an up and down rollercoaster. I didn't feel like talking to anyone. I didn't want to go out. My best friend was worried about me. I wasn't the same. I wasn't cracking any jokes or acting silly. She missed the person that I was and didn't understand the person that was in front of her, breaking down, sad, depressed and through with love. My cousin had told me that my best friend said that she didn't know what to say, that I was the one that encouraged them and knew what to do for others when they were going through. What they failed to understand was, I needed to hit rock bottom. It was necessary. I had called the cable company and gotten the cable turned off. I had a FireTVstick there was no need in making it hard on myself. I had already canceled my plan with T-Mobile and went to Family Mobile. Everything was going to get better, I knew it would. The water from the hot water heater was getting worse. I didn't have any money right then and I wasn't asking anyone for it. I depended on my refund check to take care of bills and in this case, the hot water heater was going to be the first thing I handled. I talked to my cousin Donna and she told me to report it to my homeowner's insurance company. I did and thank GOD; the damages were covered.

Severe water damage and the detection of moisture in my house allowed me to put flooring through my entire home; except for the two bedrooms. Things were finally warming up for me once.

Chapter 27

I'm single now. I'm no longer engaged and I'm not planning an October 8, 2017, wedding; red, black, and white; seven bridesmaids and seven groomsmen, flower girl, ring bearer, and I'm no longer working on getting one of my celebrity friends to sing. My gift to him was going to be a bass guitar and I had told my cousin that I wanted a Brahmin Handbag as my gift. After the reception, we were going on our honeymoon to Hawaii and putting love notes on paper to create more R&B songs. I was excited to be planning a wedding, tasting cakes, trying on dresses, and being so hands on, that I was designing my stationary. I had my cousin Ebony as the Matron of Honor, my best friend Tiffany the Maid of honor and five others were bridesmaids. I had to dismiss my best friend Wanda from being a bridesmaid because I felt she did not uphold her corner. My cousin tells me that she would not be able to be in the wedding because she and her husband were expecting a beautiful baby. I understood all of that. The day the bridesmaids met to try on their dresses at David's Bridal was a pleasant experience. Until I told one of the bridesmaid's daughter not to take pictures. I felt a little tension between us when I stated the obvious, that pictures should not be taken of what the ladies were wearing. She deleted the pics but the bridesmaid decided to let me know that she would no longer be able to get me my dress. That was her gift to me. Due to an unforeseen circumstance on a come up that didn't make it off the ground and I was okay with that. I called all the bridesmaids and maid and matron of honor letting them know that the wedding was off. Constantly crying daily. I would break down and cry in an instant. My best friend and cousin planned an outing to get me out of the house. I went but I wasn't in the mood for it. They went outside on the patio for a minute too long, so I left; driving all the way home in tears. Being in a relationship was the last thing on my mind. Yet, here he was calling my phone. I made it through the New Year and the following week I received a call from my ex-fiancé. He told me how afraid he was of me for pulling the gun out on him that he still loved me. His phone bill was coming due and I told him to use a Wi-Fi number to make calls. I even made his payment on his phone bill. For most of, many of the 5-years, we were never apart. I was used to being around him and felt I was in a place where I didn't want to be alone. I finally got my wish. I was living alone. My youngest daughter was in Durham in college and my oldest and my granddaughter had moved out. So, all the hollering and screaming, kicking I did was just between me and GOD. I even asked GOD if letting him come back was the right thing to do. HE never answered me. One day he and I were engaged in comforting conversation and him just blurted out, "Come and get me". I asked him where he was and I headed 35-minutes away to Kannapolis NC to pick him up. The weatherman was calling for snow and I told him that I didn't want to be shut in alone. We went out to eat, picked up some goodies from the store and came back to the house and watched movies and we had the best sex ever. Then it was time to go. Really? All this conversation about getting a job, starting over with me, not worrying about what others thought; here he was asking me to take him back to Kannapolis. I did and with the biggest attitude. He gathered everything that he had left behind and took it with him. I felt played. I cried like a baby because afterwards, he did not accept any more phone calls from me. I felt the rage of Carrie all up inside of me; angry, disgusted, and downright furious at the same time. It was time for me to get my shit together. I was keeping house before him and I will be alright without him. I reminded myself of who my source is and I began to slowly allow the process to navigate me in the timing necessary to grow, let go, and boss back up into the amazing woman that I am. I started going out more. Sometimes by myself. Meeting new people and even running into a few throwbacks. Every date or encounter that I had reminded me of the gentleman that my ex was. He opened car doors and pulled out chairs. Not these cats I found myself involved with after him. Absolutely no home training. I wasn't desperate to find love. I was hungry enough to find the person I lost over a 5-year time span, me. Soon getting ready to graduate from college and I was also receiving invitations to weddings. Many I turned down and one I accepted.

My cousin Jenelle was getting ready to marry the love of her life in the Spring of 2017. I went to the mall and found me a nice outfit and a pair of shoes for this joyous occasion. I arrived on time with butterflies in my stomach. I did not attend events that I knew couples would be at. I turned down a lot of invitations, because I was not ready to be asked the question, "Where is such and such?" Everything about the wedding was spectacular, down to the time and day. I was doing fine up until the bridesmaids came down the aisle. The ladies were wearing the same dresses I had picked out for my girls, just a different color. I part of me went to the wedding more for me. I love my cousin and welcome Ambrose into the family. However, this moment was a necessary push to get me further out of the funk that I was in. When I arrived at the reception, I was seated dead smack in the front of the bride and groom's table. For the most part I did fine. Until Jenelle whispered from afar, "Are you okay?" I shook my head, "Yes". Inside I was dying, pieces of my soul were unraveling and my heart was stuck in a place between love and I don't want to love no more. I made it through the wedding and the reception and I'm glad I made my way instead of denying the invitation. It was all about me. This was my turn to heal and I had a few more credit hours left and after all these years, I was getting ready to graduate.

Chapter 28

The last day of summer school at Johnson C Smith University was July 14 and I DeVondia Regina Roseborough graduated cum laude with a 3.49 GPA. It was going to be a party and I was excited about my family and friends coming together to celebrate my accomplishments. Well, everyone didn't show up and I felt a certain type of way about it but I realized those that didn't show up were not on my journey as close as the ones that were. July was bittersweet. Even though I graduated with honors, I also lost my dad 2-weeks prior to my degree arriving in the mail. Joe Kennedy was my dad, he wasn't a stepfather. He was the man that raised me and the man I didn't pay attention too until it was too late. I had already made the wrong decisions in relationships and I had a positive model right in front of me, showing me how a man treated a woman and what to expect from a man. I miss you Pop! I decided, after little convincing from one of my professors that I needed to go to grad school and I applied right here in Charlotte. I was accepted and currently working on my masters of communications arts at Queens University of Charlotte. One day I was thumbing around on my Facebook page and I saw a message from a name I was not familiar with.

Messenger: "I'm sorry" (With a crying emoji)
Me: "Who is this"

Messenger: "No disrespect, just wanted you to know that. No disrespect. I won't harass you. We need to talk". (Inserts telephone number with GA., area code).

Me: "Who is this?" I felt in my spirit it was my ex-fiancé. Where did he come from and why does he have a Georgia area code? So, my suspicions were true. I kept it to myself as I investigated. First, I went to my fake Facebook page. I went to his page to see how life was going for him. I wanted to know if he was happy. I looked to see how he was looking.

Then one day, I saw a picture of the lady that I confronted him with on Christmas Eve tagged with a caption, "Celebrating her birthday". I wasn't 100 percent sure if it were her but I snooped until I got confirmation that it was. "But it wasn't like that", let her tell it. The moment this was revealed to me, I was hurt. I cried and wondered when did he have time to cheat? Where did he find the opportunity to get away and make another woman happy? He was so far up my ass it wasn't a doubt in my mind that he pulled that stunt again. After I put the pieces together the hurt resurfaced and it cut me deeper than me putting him out and him playing me. I decided to make the call to see who this was sending me messages on my page from a profile I wasn't familiar with.

When he answered the phone and his deep

baritone voice said, "Hello beautiful". My heart melted. I recall him messaging me a couple of times from his original page, telling me how proud he was of me.

I so kindly replied, "Please do not contact me again". For some reason, I felt we needed to have this conversation. I listened to why he went to GA., and that he went down with my neighbor's aunt because she wanted to help him get his life together. He admitted having sex with her and getting kicked out and moving in with a coworker. I told him that he went down there with no responsibilities and there was no excuse why he didn't have a car and his own place. He was still the man I had put out but he claimed to still love me. We started talking on the phone early September. He told me about why he ended up losing his job and moving in with his co-worker and his lady. I asked him about my engagement ring and he said he still had it. He even said he sent my daughter a picture of it via inbox on Facebook. I won't even write what he said happened to it because so many stories had been told that I just can't with the lies right now. When he lost his job working with the coworker, the coworker's lady did not have the energy to take him back and forth to his new job. He said the lady told him that he needed to go back to the lady he went to GA with. I told him she was right. At least you will have a guaranteed ride back and forth to work and a stable place to stay.

"Since you think everyone is out to use you.

Do you. Go and make her think you are in love with her until you come up". He could not believe the words that were coming out of my mouth. Hell, I didn't either. But the truth of the matter is, we talked about getting back together but the more we talked the more GOD revealed the signs, even more, to not waste my time. He was on probation for a traffic ticket and trouble found him once again and this was the little pep talk I gave him.

"Listen, it seems since you left to go to GA., every weapon that has formed against you has prospered. You need to drop to your knees and call on the LORD. You need to seek forgiveness from all the people you have wronged, handle your business, and fall in love with you. Go to the mall and buy you some clothes and shoes and get you a pedicure like we used to do. Stop trying to please a woman when you are not pleased with yourself. I can't wait for you to get out of this situation. I can't continue bailing you out. We can be friends but nothing else".

Some other stuff popped off but let me just say, I let Ms. GA peach know my presence was near and he would always love me and that she was a nasty bitch to lie right in my face. I decided to keep my cool after that and pray, release, and move on. I blocked him and her and went on with my life. One of the easiest things I ever did. I partied like a rock star after my father died and I promised myself I would not have another drink or go out until my birthday. October 8, 2017, was my 46th birthday and scheduled wedding date. I decided that I was not going to date, talk to any men, and stay focused on what mattered. My goal was to make it through the year and start anew after Christmas Day.

Chapter 29

Oh, a sister inbox was thumping. Plenty of, "Hey lady, how are you?" "What happened to that light skin dude you were engaged to?" It was not the time for me to get involved with anyone. I promised myself, that I was going to work on me. I made me a priority this time. I knew it was time to get myself together and the thought of being in a relationship was the farthest thing from my mind. It was now my turn to do me. I cried many of days but that last conversation I had with him, gave me so much confidence, I felt a complete lifting from my body. It's the feeling you get when you have carried a lot of groceries at one time, and you finally put them down. I no longer wanted to tote anyone else's baggage. My bags were already filled and it was high time for me to empty everything that was holding me down and keeping me from walking in my purpose. I am blessed with an abundance of gifts and talents; from singing to designing marketing material, the art of facilitating, in my unique way, management, branding, being a dynamic speaker, and turned my best advice, giving self into a certified master life coach. With all of this, I have no reason to be borrowing money from my best friend. She helped me a lot and I really appreciate Tiffany Barringer for everything she blessed me with. You don't find too many people that have the longevity that we have as friends and would do what we should to make sure the other is straight. I'm asked all the time, how did I do it. How did I get over him and move past a 5-year relationship so quick? For starters, I prayed a lot. I never missed a day lifting my hands to GOD and screaming help me LORD. I would sing myself happy after praying and when I would get through, I felt a lifting of the baggage I no longer wanted to carry. I dedicated myself to me and set some strategic goals. One went on to grad school girl. I just successfully completed my first semester and I put that energy from those tears into branding my business, writing books, creating personal and professional development workshops for small business owners and aspiring authors. I tapped into my gifts and talents so they can work for me. I don't want to have to depend on my friend like I did anymore. I want to be able to write her a check, more than what she blessed me with to show my appreciation for what she did for me. I stopped entertaining the conversations and the text messages with the same lines that used to woo me with a picture attached. I even stopped blocking him. It was no need to go to his page and wonder how he's living any longer. I already prayed to GOD on his behalf and I left it there. I kept telling myself I deserved better and I convinced myself that this would not be as hard as I expect it to be. I just did it. If you ever find yourself trying to figure out if you missed any red flags, just pay attention to the very things that linger in your mind. That unction that will not go away. That feeling of something is not right. Ask GOD to power up your discernment and don't have you out here looking foolish for nobody. Not even yourself. The signs are bold and on your face. Do not ignore the fact that the red sign says stop, or the green signs say go forth and make it happen. Many people won't give the right relationship a chance because they're looking for something that's not there. The escape, the great escape takes time. The goal of this last part is to determine when you're going to break free and stay free. I stayed and went back and allowed him back into my arms because I thought I was in love. In fact, I did not love myself enough to say look, you're married and until you get your divorce I cannot be a part of something that's not pleasing to GOD and that will keep me from moving forward in my purpose. Am I embarrassed for telling this story? Not at all. My goal was to write this book, that I started in 2015 but put it down multiple times because we kept breaking up and getting back together. On this last go around he gave me his blessings and told me to publish it but don't make him out to be the bad guy. We both had our differences and I wish him much success and blessings.

Open Letter to My Daughters

Dear Pearl & Pumpkin,

This letter is to publicly express my deepest apologies for allowing you and my granddaughter Zion Nicole to witness me at my lowest points with a man I allowed into our home, that was not fit for me and I not fit for him. Camisha, I thank you for rubbing my thoughts as you hugged me many times while you wiped away tears as you saw me cry my heart and soul out over being hurt and dealing with life. You saved my life many of times, just by being in the other room. You have no idea how much you mean to me.

I exposed you and your daughter to slammed doors, broken dishes, cursing, screaming, and kicked in doors because my attitude was savage like. Be careful of the company you keep and be the company people want around.

Pumpkin, even though you were in college and were not around us that much, I thank you for helping keep the lights on when our coins were not long enough to make ends meet. You made sure you let me know, that you had me. No matter who I was with, I was the only person you were concerned about.

The day you came home and found me in tears and you cried with me on Christmas Day and told me to never go back.

"Mama I need you to be strong. I look to you for strength when I'm going through. We are going to get through this together".

Look at your Big Healthy…We did it. It's Christmas Day 2017, a year after the day I thought life was over. Baby, life has just got real.

Thank you for loving me and being the best daughters a woman could ever wish or hoped for. Make sound decisions in your relationships. Don't do what I did, do as I should have. I admire you two as the beautiful, independent women, that you were raised to be.

You are both awesome mothers and I pray for a greater connection between you two. May GOD bless us all and keep us away from men that don't have our best interest in heart and that we as women recognize the signs, red flags, and don't waste any time on escaping.

Love,

Ma

www.ingramcontent.com/pod-product-compliance
Lightning Source LLC
Chambersburg PA
CBHW022113280326
41933CB00007B/375